Introduction to
Group Treatments in Psychiatry

To the Patients and Staff at Halliwick Hospital

In 1972, Halliwick Hospital was fully integrated with Friern Hospital, as part of the New Southgate Group of Hospitals, when Halliwick Hospital was renamed Halliwick House

Introduction to Group Treatments in Psychiatry

PATRICK B. de MARE

B.A.(Cantab.), M.R.C.S., L.R.C.P., M.R.C.Psych., D.P.M.

Consultant Psychotherapist, Halliwick Hospital and St. George's Hospital, London; Founder Member and Late President of the Group Analytic Society, London

and

LIONEL C. KREEGER

M.B., B.S., M.R.C.P.(Ed.), M.R.C.Psych., D.P.M.

Consultant Psychiatrist, Paddington Clinic and Day Hospital, London; Lately Consultant Psychiatrist and Psychotherapist, Halliwick Hospital, London; Member of the Group Analytic Society, London; Associate Member of the British Psychoanalytic Society

Butterworths

ENGLAND:	BUTTERWORTH & CO. (PUBLISHERS) LTD. LONDON: 88 Kingsway, WC2B 6AB
AUSTRALIA:	BUTTERWORTHS PTY. LTD. SYDNEY: 586 Pacific Highway, 2067 MELBOURNE: 343 Little Collins Street, 3000 BRISBANE: 240 Queen Street, 4000
CANADA:	BUTTERWORTH & CO. (CANADA) LTD. TORONTO: 14 Curity Avenue, 374
NEW ZEALAND:	BUTTERWORTHS OF NEW ZEALAND LTD. WELLINGTON: 26–28 Waring Taylor Street, 1
SOUTH AFRICA:	BUTTERWORTH & CO. (SOUTH AFRICA) (PTY.) LTD. DURBAN: 152–154 Gale Street

Suggested U.D.C. Number: 616.89–085.851

ISBN 0 407 22040 2

Printed in Great Britain by
REDWOOD BURN LIMITED
Trowbridge & Esher.

Contents

Preface

We felt the need of a short introductory book on groups during our work with staff at Halliwick Hospital. There did not seem to be a satisfactory one, being comprehensive on the one hand, yet brief on the other. For this reason, we undertook to try and write such a book together, feeling that our combined experiences should justify the attempt. So often we have heard people complaining of the difficulty they were experiencing in finding the sort of book that they required. Either a book was too large and complex, or it dealt with only certain aspects of the subject, or from a particular and perhaps rigid viewpoint.

This book has been written in the hope that it will offer an attractive yet stimulating experience to those who are on, or near to, the threshold of working with groups.

One aspect of group work which has impressed itself upon us, is the degree of anxiety that invariably occurs when someone is about to expose himself to a group situation. Groups appear to be threatening in a way which does not occur in other treatment situations. It is important to realize and accept this fact, both in terms of staff and patients. It may well explain the peculiar reluctance of many to become involved in group work. Milton Berger has put it succinctly – 'Trainees (in group psychotherapy), who are not anxious must be sick.

P.B. de M.
L.C.K.

ONE

Introduction

Until recently in this country, psychiatry has been dominated by the organic approach, both in terms of the aetiology of mental illness and in its treatment. The classical approach in psychiatry related to the sway that the natural sciences of the nineteenth century held in psychology. The so-called descriptive attitude to the subject originated with Emil Kraepelin (1856–1926) who, by careful attention to the presenting phenomena of the illness, managed to classify certain specific types of psychiatric illness, namely manic-depressive psychosis, and what we now call schizophrenia. With regard to treatment, ECT (electro-convulsion therapy) was introduced in 1937, and deep insulin coma in 1938. Largactil was first used clinically in 1952, and since then there has been a flood of drugs intended for use in psychiatry; tranquillizers, anti-depressants, hypnotics, and so on.

Sigmund Freud (1856–1939) was born in the same year as Kraepelin, and through his genius opened up an entirely new area of understanding. He found the then current approach to mental illness sterile, began using hypnosis both in investigation and treatment, and later abandoned the hypnotic technique once he had demonstrated the overall superiority of the method of free-association, the foundation-stone of psychoanalysis. Freud's pioneering work has led the way to the application of psychoanalytic principles, both in individual psychotherapy and in group psychotherapy.

Thus, we start with a division between the organic and the psychodynamic approach; one which we hope is becoming less marked in recent years, but unfortunately there still are those who take up a rigid and unyielding stand in defence of the one and to attack the other. There is no doubt that what is needed at this time is an eclectic outlook, to try and view psychiatric illness in a total way, and to utilize as far as is possible, the most appropriate methods of treatment for any particular patient. This is one of the main values of group therapy. As a technique, group therapy is so flexible and versatile that it can be applied in virtually all situations.

CRITIQUE OF THE ORGANIC APPROACH

Take, for example, the now-abandoned treatment of schizophrenia, deep insulin coma. It was introduced by Sakel in the 1930s, and was hailed as the most effective way of treating schizophrenia at that time. Its use spread throughout the world and, in Great Britain, every mental hospital had its 'insulin ward'. Dutifully, the schizophrenic patients in that special unit would accept daily injections of insulin, which lowers the blood-sugar level, which in turn led to a state of unconsciousness (hypoglycaemic coma). The coma was allowed to continue for about an hour, and was eventually terminated by giving glucose by mouth or, if necessary, intravenous injection. About 30 or 40 treatments were given in all. Occasionally there were complications, such as irreversible coma, which could lead to paralysis or even death, but despite the risks, everyone accepted the value of the treatment and it was the standard method for the next 20 years or so.

In 1953 Harold Bourne wrote an article in the *Lancet* entitled 'The insulin myth', in which he questioned the validity of its effectiveness in the treatment of schizophrenia. A heated correspondence ensued in the journal, and one very eminent and senior psychiatrist began his letter as follows: 'Many will sympathise with Dr. Bourne's youthful impatience . . .' Others insisted that there was no doubt on clinical grounds that deep insulin coma was the best treatment available for schizophrenia at that time.

In 1957, Brian Ackner published his paper 'Insulin treatment of schizophrenia – A controlled study', again in the *Lancet,* and showed that there was no significant difference in outcome between two groups of schizophrenics: one treated with insulin comas, the other with comas resulting from barbiturates. Thus it was proved that the effect of insulin was non-specific, and that whatever the reason for improvement in schizophrenic patients, it was not insulin as such. This led to the virtually total abandonment of insulin in the treatment of schizophrenia.

In more recent years, phenothiazine drugs, such as Largactil, have become the standard treatment of schizophrenia, but there is now much evidence that it is the effect of relationships in hospital wards that is all-important in facilitating improvements. For instance, Dr. David Cooper in his book *Psychiatry and Anti-psychiatry,* quotes results obtained in 'Villa 21' at Shenley Hospital, which are at least as good as those obtained by more conventional treatment (that is, physical methods). In Villa 21, physical methods were not used, and it was run along therapeutic community lines, with emphasis on an existential–psychotherapeutic approach.

Again, perhaps too much adherence to the use of ECT (electro-convulsive therapy, or electric treatment), prevents the more thorough assessment of patients suffering from depression. Some psychiatrists use ECT routinely in depression, with little wish to know or understand the psychological implications of the condition. No doubt there are severely depressed cases, carrying a high suicidal risk that justify the immediate use of ECT, but on the whole these are less common than the sort of cases in which one can employ anti-depressant drugs and offer support, encouragement and the opportunity to try to obtain an understanding of what has led to the depressive reaction.

In an article entitled 'Clinical trial of the treatment of depressive illness', undertaken by the Clinical Psychiatry Committee of the Medical Research Council, and published in the *British Medical Journal* in 1965, the *long-term* (that is 24 weeks) evaluation of results was as follows:

> Approximately one-third of patients have had a satisfactory outcome on a placebo alone (22 out of 61). This figure was increased to slightly more than one-half after the exhibition of ECT alone (35 out of 65), or imipramine (Tofranil) alone (34 out of 63).

In other words, after six months of treatment of depressive illness, one-third of cases have recovered with a placebo, as against one-half with either Tofranil or ECT, and note that ECT is not superior to Tofranil in the long run. With these results in mind, perhaps one should read again Macdonald Critchley's review of ECT written in 1943, some 30 years ago. He ends as follows:

> The artificial production of convulsions as a form of therapy is crude, dangerous, and repellant to anyone who holds the central nervous system in respect. That it may for a time be the optimum available treatment is perhaps true; that it is high time to improve upon it is even truer.

So much then, for questioning the specific value of certain physical methods of treatment in psychiatry. Again, we would stress the need for an eclectic approach, but certainly one that includes the attempt to utilize psychodynamic methods.

CONTEXT

What is necessary today is a fresh approach to the whole current of psychiatric needs in dealing with the mass phenomena of mental illness, taking into account that over half the hospital beds are those taken up by the mentally disturbed. For example, there are about 5,000 actual suicides a year and many more attempted, and this, with the increase in drug addiction, confronts us with the necessity of adopting a broader and more dynamic approach. Psychoanalysis and other forms of individual psychotherapy cannot possibly cope adequately with the overall demands; for instance, the vast majority of the 350 psychoanalysts reside and work in the London area. Increasingly, we are being faced by the need for psychosocial medicine and, in a recent HMSO publication (*Psychiatric Nursing Today and Tomorrow,* 1968), it is stated 'We recommend that basic training (for nurses), should recognise the increased need for ability in communication; and, in addition to providing theoretical knowledge of group dynamics, should also, where possible, include participation in groups.'

Clearly the function of the various psychoanalytic institutes and psychotherapy training centres must be mainly to offer training in these disciplines, but as service contributions to the treatment requirements, they are but a drop in the ocean, and if the criteria for psychotherapy were to be based on the availability of facilities this could very well grossly distort the manifestation of emotional disturbances in favour of psychosomatic, psychotic, criminal, and other social expressions of conflict and unrest, e.g. drug addiction.

The problems of the therapeutic community versus community care are reaching dilemma proportions and are in urgent need of clarification and formulation. With the new concepts of community care there has arisen a rapid hospital turnover in which patients are discouraged from exploring their problems, and physical methods are applied for temporary alleviation of symptoms, so that a collusion of denial between patient and doctor over emotional factors results and the more gradual emergence of insight, understanding, which goes at a slower tempo, but is basically more radical and long-lasting, is lost sight of. The maturational processes started off in the therapeutic community setting often do not begin before several months have elapsed and six months', rather than six weeks' stay in a hospital may be necessary from our experience. The time is bound to arise when costing per person rather than per bed will have to be adopted.

Joint appointments of consultants between two or three hospital and perhaps day centres, with less time spent in each situation, makes for confusion and evasion because of lack of clinical time. Patients are referred to local authority agencies such as social workers where the pressures upon these or on the relatives of the patients may become overwhelming and will merely result in a shift of responsibility rather than an honest confrontation of the problem. This also applies to all members of the psychiatric hospital staff in that the training of the staff of a therapeutic community shows a complex and slow development requiring time and attention. It is constantly changing and often entails several years of teething troubles before becoming reasonably established.

From all these considerations, it is clear that group therapy is the main therapeutic tool available to us in the attempt to create a new psychiatric dimension. It is expedient, thoroughly practical, and also offers itself as the treatment of choice for many people suffering from mental illnesses.

AIMS OF GROUP PSYCHOTHERAPY

What is the basic purpose of group psychotherapy? What are the principles of the curative process, and the aims of this treatment method?

Different schools of group therapy have their own theoretical and technical approaches, and to attempt some background against which to explore further, perhaps we can indicate a few of these.

Foulkes and Anthony (1957) offer a broad orientation in considering the varieties and types of groups:

(1) Relief through expression and catharsis (that is, the reliving of some intense emotional experience).
(2) Restoration through participation and acceptance.
(3) Laying bare of disturbing conflicts, bringing them to awareness, the liquidation of old fixations in development, and the liberation of creative forces in the individual.

In *Small Group Psychotherapy*, edited by Walton (1971), effective treatment is said to be based on three contentions:

(1) Desired behavioural changes occur more readily with group psychotherapy than with other psychological treatments.
(2) Such changes are more enduring.
(3) People treated in groups improve their social relationships.

Yalom (1970) lists ten curative factors in group psychotherapy:

(1) Imparting of information.
(2) Instillation of hope.

(3) Universality.
(4) Altruism.
(5) Corrective recapitulation of the primary family group.
(6) Development of socializing techniques.
(7) Imitative behaviour.
(8) Interpersonal learning.
(9) Group cohesiveness.
(10) Catharsis.

This brief introduction is necessarily limited, but we hope that it succeeds in presenting some dimension to the place of group psychotherapy in the psychiatric culture of today.

REFERENCES

Ackner, B., Harris, A. and Oldham, A. J. (1957). 'Insulin treatment of schizophrenia – a controlled study.' *Lancet*, **1** 607.

Bourne, H. (1953). 'The insulin myth.' *Lancet*, **2**, 964.

Cooper, D. (1967). *Psychiatry and Anti-psychiatry*. London: Tavistock Publications.

Critchley, M. (1943). In *Medical Annual*. Bristol: John Wright.

Foulkes, S.H. and Anthony, E. J. (1957). *Group Psychotherapy*. Harmondsworth: Penguin.

Psychiatric Nursing: Today and Tomorrow (1968). London: HMSO.

Report of MRC Clinical Psychiatry Committee (1965). 'Treatment of depressive illness.' *Br. med. J.*, **1** , 881.

Walton, H. (Ed.) (1971). *Small Group Psychotherapy*. Harmondsworth: Penguin.

Yalom, I. D. (1970). *Theory and Practice of Group Psychotherapy*. New York: Basic Books.

TWO

Historical Review

The story of socio-cultural factors in human relationships is as old as recorded history, but its deliberate application in a more therapeutic sense did not begin until the turn of the century, when an American sociologist, William Cooley, first referred to the primary group as 'the nursery of human nature'. About the same time, Joseph Pratt, a chest physician, adopted group methods in the treatment of tuberculosis. Somewhat later, in 1921, it was Freud who wrote his important theoretical paper 'Group psychology and the analysis of the ego', and introduced ideas which he did not develop further in terms of group analysis; rather, one might say, he left off where group analysis began. Another psychoanalyst, Trigant Burrow, during the 1920s first adopted the term 'group analysis' and in 1931 Moreno introduced the phrase 'group psychotherapy'. These were the early days of group psychotherapy and it was not until the mid-1930s that a more deliberate attempt was made to apply group methods both more comprehensively and more intensively. Such workers as Codie Marsh, operating in relatively large social groups, applying the slogan 'By the crowd they have been destroyed; by the crowd they shall be healed', conducted mental hygiene classes. Then in the second half of the 1930s, such workers as Slavson, Wender and Schilder applied psychoanalytic concepts to small groups. Slavson, an educationalist, worked mainly with children. Wender and Schilder adopted the small lecture room setting, reading case histories of already analysed patients as a starting-off point for further discussion. Both were psychoanalysts and both were impressed by the tendency of the patients to become increasingly involved with each other and less lecturer-orientated. We must not overlook the invaluable contributions made by the micro-functionalists in sociology, in particular Kurt Lewin, who coined the term 'group dynamics' in 1939. In this context, it is relevant to appreciate that Cooley, Lewin, Lawrence K. Frank, and many others, were in fact social psychologists, foreshadowing the new mode of a psychological element that is today playing a progressively more important role in community therapy.

So far these developments originated mainly in the United States, although in England there was quite an actively developing interest in so-called Adlerian groups. Indeed, one of us (P.B.de M.), belonged to a small society which investigated these phenomena both in London and at Cambridge during the late 1930s. Joshua Bierer was instrumental in introducing the first social club at Runwell Hospital, and later he established the first day hospital, The Marlborough Day Hospital. In 1946 he also established the Institute of Social Psychiatry in whose charter a new term 'social psychiatry' was first mentioned.

The next big move in group therapy was ushered in by the impetus of psychiatry in World War II when a technique was urgently needed to cope with the mass demands of psychiatric breakdown amongst the troops. At the end of World War I the War Office had recommended a substantial provision of psychiatrists to deal with the shell shock cases in the future. However, in the early days of World War II there was only a handful of psychiatrists equipped to handle the shoals of battle exhaustion cases, as they were then described. The problem did not arise in the German Army since they dealt with these cases summarily, by execution. The outcome was that some 400 psychiatrists were deployed throughout the services. Several hospitals were delegated for this purpose including Northfield Hospital which was to become one of the most active centres that has yet existed in the development of group techniques.

Foulkes, Bion, Rickman and Main were all officers at Northfield and were actively involved in the promotion of small group, ward group and total hospital milieu or community techniques and they had a profound influence on psychiatry throughout the army; for example, the War Office Selection Boards were run on group lines by Rickman and Bion, and in due course this approach was adopted by other allied forces such as the Americans, so that here and in the United States, demobilization resulted in the dissemination of these ideas throughout the more progressive elements in psychiatry generally. For example, Bion was appointed to the Tavistock Clinic, Foulkes to the Maudsley, and Main to the Cassel. Maxwell Jones, who had been in the Emergency Medical Service, created the Social Rehabilitation Unit which was later to become the Henderson Hospital. One of us (P.B.de M.), was fortunate in working at Northfield, and saw at first hand the history of these developments.

Let us turn now to the post-war developments of group psychotherapy in this country. Essentially there have been two main trends; the approach developed at the Tavistock Clinic and Foulkes' work at the Maudsley. At the Tavistock Clinic, Bion and Ezriel, amongst others, based their concepts on Kleinian constructs – the paranoid and depressive positions and projective identification; the 'here and now', the common group tension and the basic assumptions (see Glossary).

Foulkes, on the other hand, developed an approach which he has called group analytic psychotherapy in which emphasis is made on the group itself and its specific group features. In other words, it becomes an instrument which in due course learns how to treat itself, where the total communicational network, namely the group matrix, is regarded as a central dynamic factor in therapy. His is a rather more developmental approach as far as the group itself is concerned.

Various training programmes exist for those wishing to acquire group skills, for example at the Tavistock Clinic and Institute of Human Relations, and the Institute of Group Analysis, which is linked to the Group Analytical Society of London. The Institute of Group Analysis offers a range of training experience, from a General Group Work Course designed as an introduction to the field, to the recently formed Qualifying Course in Group Psychotherapy, intended to provide a full and comprehensive training programme for selected candidates.

In the United States there has been considerable expansion during the post-war period and again two main trends can be deciphered. First, that of Moreno and his followers, all of whom have been influenced by sociological concepts and have developed along the lines of sociology and psychodrama, as distinct from Slavson and others who placed greater emphasis on the interplay of psychoanalytic and group dynamic concepts. In fact there has been a marked pendular swing between those who emphasize the individual and psychoanalytic dynamics and those who, on the other hand, place greater importance on group aspects. Of the former, Slavson, Alexander Wolf and Schwarz are representative; Wolf for instance, who began therapeutic groups in his private practice in New York in 1938, and published his findings in 1949, undertook what he termed 'psychoanalytic groups', underpinned by the four basic tenets of psychoanalysis, namely dream interpretation, free association, analysis of resistance and transference.

Other important contributions to group therapy have come from the Gestalt psychologists, particularly Fritz Perls, from Games Theory, and from the Encounter movement, such as the Esalen Institute in California. The School of Behavioural Psychology, based on Learning Theory, is also applying its own particular techniques in group situations.

To return to developments in Britain, the recent formation of the Royal College of Psychiatry is an indication of the wider acceptance of the discipline of psychiatry in its own right. For some years, the Royal Medico-Psychological Association persisted in its attempts to obtain a supplemental charter, and eventually in June 1971, was successful in being granted the necessary Royal Charter for its metamorphosis into the Royal College of Psychiatry. Considerable thought and planning has gone into its creation, including the question of training in psychotherapy, both for general psychiatrists and specialized psychotherapists. Psychiatric Hospitals have applied for accreditation, so that they may be recognized as being suitable for trainees to work there in order to fulfill their training obligations. Part of their general experience must include practical and theoretical work in psychotherapy, both individual and group. The provision of group psychotherapeutic training facilities is of tantamount importance. As yet there are comparatively few hospitals in a position to undertake such training, but with the emphasis now being placed on the value of group experience it is inevitable that further expansion in this field will occur.

A parallel of this is shown in the increasing interest in psychosocial nursing as reflected in such publications as the HMSO review *Psychiatric Nursing, Today and Tomorrow,* which clearly recommends that all psychiatric nurses should have experience of group work as part of their basic training. In the *British Medical Journal* (June 1969) there was a leading article entitled 'Who should do psychotherapy?' which takes up the whole question of the provision of psychotherapeutic facilities, when again the matter of non-medical involvement in psychotherapy is considered.

The Seebohm Report recommended sweeping changes in the Social Services which have affected the entire tenor of social psychiatry, with the development of a psychosocial dimension towards community therapy which included the setting up of day centres, hostels and social clubs.

These are some of the changes which will greatly influence the practice of psychiatry in the immediate future and the history of which we have here outlined, whose way has been paved from these modest beginnings.

THREE

Group Structures

The groups which concern us here are all those which are met with in the course of psychiatric treatment generally, whatever the specific form of treatment might be, whether organic or psychotherapeutic, whether as a secondary background factor or as a primary agent; in either case group relational features play a significant role and it is our intention to scrutinize and use these factors deliberately and with full awareness, rather than leaving them to chance or to fortuitous and largely unconscious pressures, since these might well hinder rather than promote progress in therapy.

Generally speaking the types of group we encounter in the treatment situation can be usefully formulated under the three interwoven aspects of *group structure, group process* and *group content;* in other words the event of the group itself, its actions and its meaning.

In this chapter we shall be dealing mainly with group structures and will only pass cursorily over process and content since we shall be returning to them subsequently.

GROUP STRUCTURE

Group structure concerns matters of: (*a*) group occupation, and (*b*) group organization.

Group Occupation

Group occupation concerns the declared goal or purpose of the group – its ostensible and professed task or work, for which purpose it meets in the first place. It has been included under structure since function and structure are mutually interlinked. These range from such activities as free-floating discussions without any set topic, to highly organized occupations. Inevitably the activity determines the appropriate structuring; for instance, in non-directive discussion groups the seating is best arranged in a circle as distinct from a semi-circle of the speaker centred lecture setting.

Taking into account that there is considerable spectrum overlap, the group occupations vary from intensively psychotherapeutic procedures, such as the free-floating discussion of group association, to less directly personal situations, such as ward meetings; finally to occupational and recreational activities. One must bear in mind that in the psychiatric situation, these activities do not constitute aims in themselves, but carry an ultimate therapeutic intent in which emotional experience, communication, relationship, information flow and insight all play a primary role.

Let us look at group occupation from three aspects: namely, that of the psychotherapeutic, from the communicational and from the recreational and occupational.

(1) The *psychotherapeutic* group specifically concerns groups where people meet and talk with the object of gaining insight and understanding of their psychological conflicts and emotional and relational problems. Obviously there is no clear-cut line between communication and psychotherapy since the primary aim of psychotherapy is to understand the implications and, therefore, the meanings of ostensibly nonsensical and meaningless symptoms, rather like the factor of noise in cybernetics. This is what is meant by 'insight', which forms in the last resort the cornerstone of dynamic psychiatry. The paradigm of psychotherapeutic groups, for instance, where group-analytic psychotherapy is practised, is the small group, which will be described at greater length in subsequent chapters; however, we would emphasize here that we do not confine these deepening personal insights to the small group situation alone, since the larger settings of ward, social club and community, offer their own characteristic media and idioms for promoting social insight.

(2) This brings us to the second heading, that of *communicational* and informational groups where the venues are more directly involved with verbal exchanges as distinct from the occupational groups, but less so than the psychotherapeutic groups. Everyday ordinary existence is characterized by people talking to each other more or less freely and the importance of this form of exchange is often overlooked until an untimely nervous breakdown dramatically reveals the hidden factors of increasing isolation that have been going on often over a lengthy period prior to the eventual hospitalization. The hospital should provide an

atmosphere and the facilities for people to feel encouraged and free to re-discover, indeed discover, perhaps for the first time, better ways of relating. The ability of patients to develop this will very greatly depend on the capacity of the staff to promote this, not least by *their* ability to provide something of a model with which the patients can identify.

If communication is bad at staff level, if the staff are split, this is inevitably reflected and amplified by the patients. Rigidly hierarchical and one-way communication from above downwards amongst the staff, destroys their ability to achieve a flexible, fluent informational system which in turn creates a similar problem for the patients. This can be improved by establishing staff meetings at all, and of all, levels, staff, committee, cross shift, and total community, involving all staff and patients, and a similar parallel system is established amongst the patients in the form of ward and community meetings, discussion groups, and the total community meetings which include the staff.

(3) Under the last heading, that of *recreational and occupational* groups, the emphasis is – in contrast to the analytic groups which have no set task – on the activity itself which acts as a catalyst for promoting interaction, an excuse, as it were, to provoke association and contact amongst the participants.

In the recreational groups the fact that in the normal course of events people get together for amusement, is taken up and applied with therapeutic intent. It has been said that reality is moulded by small talk and it has been noticed that trivial conversations and exchanges and common place interaction is conspicuous by its absence in long-stay wards of mental hospitals. Institutionalization leads to impoverishment of just this type of interplay. Recreation revives and encourages contact, provides stimulus, and is an essential feature of rehabilitation; apparently meaningless and inconsequential events may have the significance of enabling people to start making 'a new beginning', and pleasurable response may be as relevant as any entered record of a patient's progress.

Occupational activities on the other hand tend to be of a more ambitious nature, are more established and less spontaneous, and involve projects of all sorts ranging at one end from the recreational, from the more creative such as music, art or craft, to work-centred activities such as cooking or industrial therapy programmes at the other. Again, it is not so much the activities and tangible productions themselves which are primary; rather it is the emphasis on the promotion of relationships and the increased tolerance required in relating which is regarded as therapeutic since many of the patients will have broken down precisely over these tensions in the group settings at their work and other situations.

Group Organization

Group organization concerns matters of size; selection; and general arrangements – how many? who? when? and where?

Size

The size of the group is a crucial factor and is influenced by a number of variables including function, activity, environment and facilities of all sorts. The early sociologists, Durkheim for instance, were much taken up with matters of group number and the manner in which number affects and is affected by group function. Three people is usually regarded as the minimal number constituting a group. Less than three constitutes the one-to-one relationship which is the province of individual psychotherapy and psychoanalysis. At the other end of the scale are the global groups of the community at large, of community therapy (as distinct from the therapeutic community), and of hospital regions, catchment areas, which are beyond our present terms of reference, but which in the form of psychosocial media and the large group are going to play an increasingly important role in the future.

Groups may be classified as small, medium and large:

(1) *Small groups* range from three to ten members. Psychotherapeutic groups almost universally, by general agreement and empirical experience, consist of seven to eight members. Groups of below this number, e.g. three to four members, are exemplified by marital and family groups.

(2) *Medium sized groups,* e.g. 10 to 30, are typified by ward meetings, staff meetings, seminars and training, or 'T-groups', and many of the activities – art, music, drama – have a tendency to settle at a membership of 9 to 12 members.

(3) *Large groups* range from 30 to 100 and are exemplified by community meetings, social clubs, and the total community in the form of the therapeutic community.

There seems to be some prejudice from both staff and patients generally against these larger gatherings; despite the fact that they form an essential aspect of any hospital network and make for the creation of a good or bad atmosphere, and of morale which in turn influences profoundly the smaller group activities, there is a tendency to evade the large meetings unless confrontation of this problem is faced up to. The reason for this is by no means clear; on the whole the literature on this aspect of the work remains comparatively limited. Perhaps there is a primary fear or feeling of alienation concerning the larger group, that they are liable to be less controllable or controlling and, therefore, are seen as more threatening. (The Anglo-Saxon word 'assembly' is derived from a word meaning 'thing'.) It is striking to read the writings of the earlier sociologists and psychologists concerning the crowd, e.g. Freud, Le Bon. They are couched in derogatory or ironic terms, of the rabble in panic or violence, alternatively of the rigidly structured large organizations such as the army or the church; there is a tacit assumption that the large groups inevitably remain on the brink of the barbaric and dehumanized. The group therapist, on the other hand, looks on a group as capable of developmental processes, given the opportunity, and that group behaviour can undergo maturational phases.

Selection

Selection is a subject on its own and here we shall only cursorily scrutinize some of the essentials in selection procedure. In essence, the smaller and the more intensive a group, the more specific must selection be. Generally speaking, it is the personality as a whole that plays the vital role as distinct from diagnostic categories or the symptomatic manifestations themselves. The question the group therapist has constantly to ask himself is can such and such a person avail himself of the facilities offered by any particular group situation? He has also to reverse the question and ask whether such and such a group situation can contain or cope with, or do justice to, the patient concerned; who is suitable for whom?

Symptom manifestations play a secondary role to the primary consideration of the total personality, and the extent to which a person can function in a social situation. The more disturbed a person, the more this can be compensated for by successful group functioning; for instance, a borderline psychotic may be able to make more use of, and give more to, a group than a person heavily weighted on the side of his neurotic defences. Selection, therefore, should be based on group functions rather than upon symptom formations, and it is for this reason that some people employ a procedure of selection by a preliminary group meeting.

The larger groups, such as the ward meetings and the hospital as a whole, do not have to be so highly selective and can include a greater variety of personalities; there can be a far wider range in such variables as age, intelligence, education, employment, career, capacity to verbalize, degrees of sophistication, colourfulness and of disturbance. Generally speaking, in the small groups there should be closer distances between those features – the groups should be relatively homogeneous – whilst in the larger groups variety and heterogeneity are not only inevitable but are preferable as being more life-like. However, it is more a question of discovering the optimum – a powerful, destructive personality can create havoc in a large group and cause such endless delays, hold-ups and fragmentations as to be wasteful and even anti-therapeutic. At the other end of the scale one might say that no one is ultimately unfit for participation in a group, provided such a group, possibly a more specialized one, can be made available.

Selection on the grounds of symptomatology, for instance mixing people whose presenting symptoms may be obsessional with hysterical or schizoid features, is a more specialized and less understood field – a 'borderline' disturbance may very well have a creative and loosening effect on a tightly conformist group but a group of depressives may 'sink the boat'. Some sort of homeostatic balance or steady state has to be achieved and it is far easier to establish this on grounds of the total personalities of the people concerned rather than on symptomatic categories. Symptoms, after all, are a form of camouflage and as such are not intended to be understood; rather they cause mystification – why, therefore, base selection on disguise? In any case they become shed in the course of treatment, and give way to more appropriate forms of expression, which constitutes the very essence of any psycho-therapeutic process.

General Arrangements

General arrangements concern the spatio-temporal matters of where and when. Like all matters concerning structure it is primarily the therapist's and staff's responsibility to arrange them in such a way as to promote these therapeutic processes. For example, there was no point in having a large glass fish tank in the middle of the lounge where the community held its meetings, as was the case at one time at Halliwick, since it obstructed visual contact and communication. More generally speaking, the architectural structure of the psychiatric hospital is itself a vital but neglected subject. Seating arrangements and general accommodation are crucial aspects; everything should be done to see that these facilities facilitate rather than hinder communication.

In the meetings themselves unpunctuality and absenteeism may be disguised resistances against exchange and change therefore, and have to be recognized as such. In order for people to be able to see each other seating arrangements are usually circular but once a meeting exceeds 30, tiered seating accommodation becomes necessary since it is impossible for people to hear each other at greater distances. The question of a chairman and agenda has to be considered in these larger settings particularly initially, but are considered as unnecessary structural defences in the smaller psychoanalytic groups. Sub-groups in the small rigorously psychoanalytic type of group are discouraged as a form of resistance or, rather, they need to be uncovered and their meaning understood; in the larger groups, however, they are an inevitable part of the community and occur spontaneously and valuably as a sociological feature of the group's attempt to consolidate the emerging of new subcultural developments.

Arrangements then play an important role in the therapeutic setting and these details should not be overlooked as they often contribute an important disguise for resistances and need to be under constant review, rather than being accepted at face value; at best they are easily neglected in matters that should be handled constructively towards our therapeutic aim of facilitating and encouraging exchange and interaction, of establishing a framework where this can unobtrusively take place.

Duration and frequency of meetings are important aspects of group organization. At Halliwick the small groups typically meet once, twice or three times weekly and last for 1¼ to 1½ hours. Ward meetings are daily and the community meeting is usually once weekly. Staff meetings occur twice a week. The Social Club meets weekly.

GROUP PROCESS

Group process concerns the actual processes of communicating, the dynamic actions and interactions that are set into motion once the structure or context of the group has been established, the movement of the group as it were, the essential 'group dynamics'. These are mediated, as we have described, through a continuum of non-verbal currencies at one end of the scale, e.g. occupational therapy, music, art, dancing, encounter, to the highly articulate verbal communications that occur in the intensive analytically-orientated psychotherapeutic groups at the other. Whilst in the creating of a rewarding group structure, the therapist plays a deliberate and active role, in relationships to the group processes his role is more passive, more 'catalytic'. His role here is neither to push the processes, nor to have to be dragged along by them; rather he walks beside them. He does not create them – they occur spontaneously provided the necessary structures are made available, and it is up to him to adopt an enabling attitude, to help facilitate these processes and to avoid swamping their spontaneous emerging by premature interventions or blocking their progress by over-interpreting or mis-interpretation, or failing to provide facilities and equipment for the activity groups.

Communication can be typed also according to the number of people involved. When it is purely personal, as in self-analysis, and in the development of insight, it can be described as intrapersonal and takes the form of monologue; when it involves two people as in individual psychotherapy and psychoanalysis, it takes the form of interpersonal dualogue and when it is between more than two people, it becomes transpersonal or dialogue, a process adopted for instance by the Greeks when discussions took place in small groups over meals, or whilst strolling around, from which the word peripatetics has been derived.

GROUP CONTENT

Group content emerges out of the previous two categories of structure and process in the form of patterns or constellations of relationships and their meaning for the participants, the result of interaction, the message that is conveyed, the outcome or meaning or context of the total experience for the individual concerned, for meaning in the final resort is always individual and personal. The group *per se* does not think or experience; it is the individual who does both. In the final resort, too, it is the group content that completes the real aim and object of the whole procedure, to make sense out of the nonsense of neurosis by uncovering its meaning in terms of relationship with others, by making aware, by making conscious, what a person is 'really' doing and being in the social context, to discover also, through choice, alternative and more appropriate ways of reacting to others. The group experience then, for the individual, can replace neurotic manifestations by posing alternatives and discovering new ways, and in that sense each group offers the possibility of being a creative phenomenon, to discover for the first time.

The conductor's function in this aspect, namely of group content, is less active than in either of the previous two for he refrains from interfering with the choice that the group makes in deciding what interest and topics to follow up, what to do, what to talk about.

Group structure, process and content bear a significant relationship to the time parameter in that structure relates also to matters that are in a sense established, past or communicated – whilst process refers to a present process of communicating. Content refers more to the potential or to the communicable future, that is, to meaning.

One way of conceptualizing the individual's contribution to the content of group functioning, is to consider the diagrammatic representation of the 'Johari window', originated by Joe Luft and Harry Ingham ('Joe and Harry', hence 'Johari') *(Figure 3.1)*.

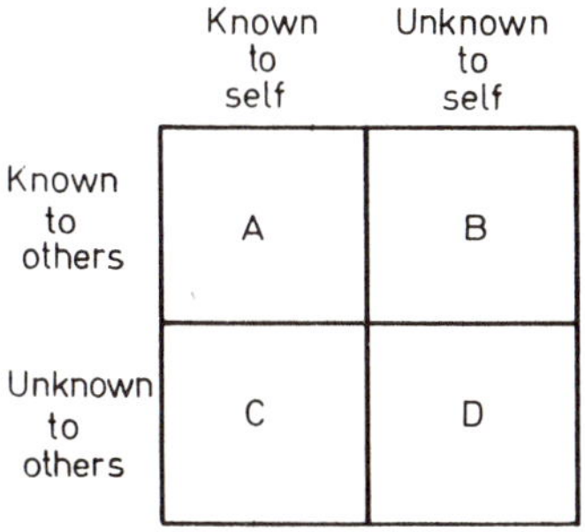

Figure 3.1

Box A (known to self, known to others) represents the 'public area' of the self.

Box B (unknown to self, but known to others) is the individual's 'blind area', which can be reduced by the process of feedback from others, such as occurs in 'T' or training groups.

Box C (known to self, but unknown to others) is the 'secret area', which can be modified by self-disclosure.

Box D (unknown to self, unknown to others) may be regarded as the 'unconscious' part of the mind, the main target for analytic understanding within a therapeutic group.

This paradigm is a beautifully concise aid to the clarification of the contributions of the individual within the group.

REFERENCE

Luft, J. (1966). *Group Processes: An Introduction to Group Dynamics.* Palo Alto: National Press.

FOUR

Practical Approaches To Groups

We are taking as our model the setting of a 100-bedded psychiatric unit with in-patient, out-patient and day hospital facilities. The main types of groups that we are likely to meet with in this setting can be classified under the following headings: (*a*) community meeting; (*b*) ward meeting; (*c*) small groups; and (*d*) staff groups.

THE COMMUNITY MEETING

Ideally, this should consist of the whole of the hospital, all the patients and all the staff. Unfortunately, such a massive mutual confrontation meets with resistances from all sources which are usually couched in highly rationalistic terms – for example, difficulty in arranging a mutually convenient time and place of meeting. If any setting could be said to show most clearly the morale of the hospital as a whole, the community meeting, its attendance and the general atmosphere gauges more accurately and revealingly than any other the true state of affairs prevailing in the community. Needless to say, the very heart of the matter is that neurosis in this context is being viewed as the outcome of a social versus a psychological discrepancy and, in a sense, the question is being begged, since a community of this sort displaying what one could consider in terms of having a high morale, is basically not likely to be constituted by people requiring treatment.

In our experience the status and the efficacy of the community project fluctuates widely, from time to time, ranging from non-existence or small desultory gatherings to large thorough-going, even inspiring, situations in which a number of factors, emotional interaction, informational exchange, atmosphere and decision-making play their roles.

In practice at Halliwick the community meeting takes place in the large lounge. All staff and patients are expected to attend since vital matters concerning the whole administration of the hospital are discussed openly. Administrative decisions can be adopted at various levels elsewhere, e.g. the staff or patients' committees, but it is the community meeting itself which provides the opportunity of acting as a sounding board for the voicing of everything that occurs, or could occur, within the hospital; it forms a good setting for the promotion, ventilation and clarification of various issues; future plans of action are decided. Considerable sensitivity is required in order to make the greatest use of gauging whether decisions have to be implemented, organized, discussed further or interpreted depending on the experience, sophistication and awareness of both patients and staff. Anybody, but anybody, can make interpretations. Here also is learned what constitutes a rewarding intervention and what is a therapeutic approach to the problems of the community as a whole. One sees clearly a panorama of the inter-relationship of all events occurring within the hospital, and that apparently minor events occurring somewhere in the hospital affect the whole network or matrix throughout its entirety which can be located against the context of this background. The community meeting has been taken first since it defines the boundaries of the total hospital setting viewed as a unit.

THE WARD MEETING

Whilst in smaller units up to 50, for instance, as at the Henderson Hospital, the community meeting takes place daily and the ward meeting weekly; with larger numbers the community meeting tends to become unwieldy and therefore the onus of responsibility has to some extent to be shifted from the community meeting to that of the various wards; ward meetings begin to take over in importance and provide a more therapeutically contained situation. This shows itself in the need for more frequent ward meetings which ideally should be daily and conveniently at the beginning of each day, say at 9.30 a.m.

Here is a setting in which an opportunity is provided for any and every patient in the ward to express feelings, problems, and ask questions, in the presence of other members, both patients and staff. At Halliwick there are about 30 patients per ward and the attendant staff present at the meetings averages half a dozen. The degree of structuring will depend on the orientation of the staff, on the type and relative sophistication of the patients, and the length of stay. Obviously, a short-stay, quick turnover membership will be relatively staff-centred as the latter constitute the regular, permanent, and, therefore, more experienced participants and (perhaps unfortunately), sometimes forms the basis of the group matrix. Like an experienced conductor in the small group therapy, the staff learn to walk beside the emerging self-awareness of the ward members, having neither to push nor pull but rather to gauge the needs of the group as a whole, which varies continuously from moment to moment. In this there does seem to be an optimal momentum for every group which can be established once the therapists have developed an awareness of the relative strengths of the members' involvement.

A patient chairman may be considered desirable and if available can bridge the gap between patients and staff and help moderate a situation in which a staff/patient division could so easily occur and provoke unnecessary hostility. There are times when it is clearly helpful to enlist the support of a chairman whose interventions will be more generally accepted and better formulated in the interests of the patients. Alternatively, the chairman can inhibit the spontaneity and distort the group feeling and indeed even encourage passivity and dependency. A patient elect may have some difficulty himself in tolerating such manifestations as silence which may in fact be valuable.

The subjects discussed at the ward meetings range from the mundane matters of hospital and ward administration – for example, the detailed arrangements for a forthcoming social evening, or the hour that patients should return to the hospital in the evenings – to the open expression of personal problems, often intimate ones, and of relationships between the members which provokes a general discussion of the kind usually associated with the smaller type of psychotherapeutic discussion group.

At a staff level, what invariably happens, to begin with, is a hierarchical type of structure with a pecking order response, and it is only as the staff become more secure that the sophistication of affiliative communication amongst the staff generally begins to manifest itself, making spontaneous, critical contributions possible rather than their remaining silently obsequious. For example, a junior member will make comments after the meeting which he felt he was not entitled to do at the main meeting itself and has, accordingly, to be encouraged to do so. David Clark has pointed out that it is the person nearest to the patient, often another patient, who is able to make the most helpful contributions since it is he who is in closest touch with what is currently going on.

Is the ward meeting group psychotherapy, or is it something quite different? Is it a social phenomenon; is it a small group process taking place in front of a larger audience; a silent Greek chorus; or has it its own distinct idiom? Flexibility must be retained at all costs to maintain spontaneity and liveliness unhampered by contrived or pre-conceived notions and interpretations. The ward is learning to converse. A characteristic of the ward meeting is that the developments of the group have no clear-cut beginning or end since there is a continuous movement, a persisting middle phase, determined by the admission and the discharge of patients to the ward, and the group is repeatedly being re-started. It often happens that for several weeks a ward group has been communicating at a relatively coherent and deep level but with the entry of a newcomer or newcomers the theme may be broken. However, with the continuity of the staff, and, to a lesser extent, of the linking by patients, a type of what might be called 'ward atmosphere and culture' emerges.

SMALL GROUPS

The principles of small group psychotherapy deserve a chapter of their own and will therefore be discussed more fully in Chapter 6. Suffice it to say here that the techniques of small group therapy that have emerged throughout Europe and the United States since the late 1930s have shown in certain aspects a surprising similarity, namely (*a*) they usually have a membership of three to ten people which often turns out to be seven or eight; (*b*) preferably they adopt a circular seating arrangement and the conductor is seated as part of the circle; (*c*) they last between one and one-and-a-half hours and meet at weekly intervals; (*d*) the approaches may range widely from a highly structured, to a relatively unstructured, unprogrammed, non-directed, free-floating discussion which will depend on the self-determined function of the group, together with the attitudes of the conductor; for instance, the small intensive psychotherapeutic group on the one hand to the spontaneous informal gatherings of members of the art hut or music group on the other. The question of size is important here since people may be able to express themselves more freely in this relatively intimate setting. In the larger meetings, the individual may find himself lost, particularly at first and in the smaller group the cliché-ridden speaker of the larger meeting may find himself encountering a closer scrutiny. The idiom and specific features of the different sized groups are quite characteristic but require further working out and understanding. The conductor may find that the smaller group can more easily be gauged as a whole, in contrast to the often less-definable and more emotive behaviour in the larger meetings.

The spectrum of activities, as we have already mentioned, ranges from the intensively psychotherapeutic at one end of the continuum to the almost purely task, work, or goal-centred project groups, such as sub-committees, at the other. There is a wide intermediary range of what have been designated T-groups, namely goal-centred groups with awareness of, or sensitivity to, relationships, emotions and insight. For instance, in a long-stay ward of a large mental hospital caring for the more profoundly disturbed, perhaps deteriorated patients, it would be inappropriate to try and apply the principles of intensive small group psychotherapy but rather in that case it would be wise to make use of the currency of occupational or recreational activities with emphasis upon encouraging elementary socialization and morale. On the other hand, in a ward treating patients suffering from basically more neurotic conflicts and selected as able to make use of a psychotherapeutic setting, small intensive psychotherapeutic groups are appropriate.

Staff attitudes are paramount in determining the choice of activities adopted, which will be elaborated later in the section on staff groups.

To list the more commonly employed types of small group we have first the *task group,* in which a commonly shared task is used as a good way of initiating and promoting the right sort of setting and atmosphere for spontaneous involvement with each other, and also for generating enthusiasm and creative endeavour. With the successful completion of the task, the sense of achievement and the appreciation of the value of shared contributions, of interest in each other, and the stimulus provided by the social situation, confronts the obstacles of the role played by the neurotic position and highlights unhelpful attitudes. This reveals neurosis as a problem of the group, acting like a sounding board which indicates in a telling way the true meaning that neurosis has in impeding relatedness in a social setting and brings back the problem to where it really belongs.

The task per se is not of primary importance but rather the role it plays in these transactions between people; commonly used activities include art, music, drama and dancing. Art therapy can be an invaluable way of enabling people to paint symbolically experiences they may not be able to express in any other form. They paint what they cannot see, the artistic merit in that case being irrelevant. Painting can be used to further understanding in much the same way as dream material. The work of interpreting can be done either by the psychotherapist or by a skilled art therapist in a small group setting. Patients can come together in a small group at the end of an art session and show their work to each other, expressing their own ideas and associations and inviting spontaneous comments. For example, a depressed patient painted a black box containing a few grey amorphous shapes. She associated to her feelings of emptiness and deadness which allowed the others to empathize verbally in terms of their own feelings of despair and depression over recent bereavements. Subsequently her paintings became more colourful and enriched as her clinical condition improved, which gave every appearance of being related to this experience.

Group interaction in music therapy is inherent and ranges from free expression on the various types of instruments such as drums and recorders to the encouragement of forming small groups and the development of more expert musicianship. For example, three patients who were shy and withdrawn, formed a pop group which is now being regularly booked for professional performances.

The place of psychodrama *per se* has not, in our experience, been sufficiently explored. However, there is always a continuous spontaneous psychodrama going on in most group situations which demands interpretation and must certainly not be overlooked, for they represent important non-verbal ways of communicating. There is plenty of scope in any therapeutic community for this type of approach. Very briefly, a group of patients may re-enact a particular experience of one of its members with encouragement to express the associated feelings which can then be followed by a fuller discussion.

Dancing can take the form of free expression or of some formal style. The latter is a self-evident and universal way of making social contact, and needs no further comment. The former, on the other hand, is a rather more specialized technique involving a trained teacher; it appears to have a distinctly liberating and freeing effect on the movement of stiff and tense patients.

Secondly, as distinct from these task-orientated groups, are the small *psychotherapeutic groups* which have the following characteristics: they usually consist of six to eight people seated round a table with the therapist as part of the circle; a non-directive attitude which implicitly encourages spontaneous and free-floating discussion and conversation when the topics are not confined and where there are no subjects which have either to be avoided or necessarily discussed. The conductor or therapist, as he is usually called, does not lead, as in other groups, and no other occupation or agenda other than the encouragement of conversation is prescribed. The point is being made that the primary contribution of group therapy lies in the value of the group situation itself as a therapeutic agent with the emergence of specifically group features.

The decision has to be made as to which of these features are therapeutic and which are not. On the whole, the general experience seems to be that free-floating discussions are helpful and that actually talking and communicating are of themselves therapeutic. In addition, a more rigorous examination of group dynamics *per se* can be practised. Alternatively, interpretation of group behaviour based on a recognized analytic approach can be undertaken, when the subtle interplay between group dynamics and psychodynamics can be explored.

The third type of group we can describe as *special groups* whose functions are both task- and psychotherapy-orientated. There are very many varieties of these groups which arise from certain specific settings; for instance, marital problems, conjoint family groups, adolescent difficulties, spontaneously formed sub-groups of all kinds, for example, people about to be discharged, or groups, which as Maxwell Jones has described, arise in crisis situations, groups which arise spontaneously from environmental pressures and which if one is alive to them can be turned to therapeutic advantage; the human networks which form in a hospital of this sort play an important role and we have hardly begun to give them the emphasis they deserve and they can only too easily be discounted and overlooked. For example, a group of some seven people was recently formed by a PSW consisting of members, all of whom were about to be discharged and were having difficulties is arranging accommodation; their joint efforts not only helped fortuitously in a tangible, practical sense but also confronted them with, and helped them resolve, the inter-personal difficulties which had played a crucial role in bringing them into the hospital in the first place. To look more closely at particular settings the most outstanding in recent years have been the conjoint family and marital groups.

Conjoint Family Groups

In has been increasingly recognized that the disturbed patient – and often an adolescent is involved – is a direct outcome of family conflict and failures in communication where conflict seems to be generated at the very source of the family itself. The role of the double bind is an example, in which, as it was originally described, the child's parents seemingly manifest gross inconsistencies in their contact with the child; for example, they say one thing but imply another, without possibility of escape from the conflict induced; e.g. 'Come and give your mother a kiss', and them turn away when the child responds.

R. D. Laing described the 'elected' sick member who contains the family illness. Examples of this are seen frequently in such instances as parents whose stormy relationship in the distant past has been replaced by a florid disturbance in the child in the present. In the course of discussions, which do not necessarily have to be very frequent (once a fortnight over a period of three months is often quite sufficient), the earlier problems re-appear and, if recognized, can result in startling improvements in the patient. When it becomes clear that it is the setting rather than any particular member that requires attention, conjoint family groups can also be formed from members of two or three small families not only as a result of expedience – for instance, when some of the members refuse to attend – but also in the added dimensions of families viewing each other in a social setting.

Marital Groups

Marital therapy can take various forms; for instance, one partner of the marriage and a therapist and the other partner with another therapist. The marital couple may be seen together in interview with one therapist. Alternatively, three or four couples can meet together in a marital group, with a therapist, or two co-therapists. The aim is not primarily to perpetuate the marriage but to clarify and elucidate the relationships and underlying conflicts in such a way as to confront mutually the emergent transference relationship within the marriage which becomes evident within the social setting of the therapeutic group. Often, this leads to strengthening of the marriage, but sometimes the only logical conclusion is for the couple to separate, each going their own way.

STAFF GROUPS

If priority were given to any particular group in the setting of the therapeutic community the staff meetings would, in our opinion, head the list.

Staff groups take the following forms.

Administrative

The primary functions of the administrative meetings are communication and exchange of information, decision and policy-making, and include such groups as the ward staff meetings. Where there is a shift system in operation a cross-shift meeting, when all the staff in contact with a patient can meet together, is essential. In all the branches of hospital administration, meetings will naturally occur – for example, medical committees, nursing staff meetings, etc – but in addition it is important for the meetings to take place between the various disciplines to ensure the promotion of free communication interdisciplinarily at all levels and to flatten the hierarchical pyramid. At Halliwick we have a weekly general staff meeting to which all members of staff are encouraged to attend. These usually contain up to 30 people and are conducted on a free-floating discussion basis with minimal directives from a chairman.

All these ways of working require a certain skill tempered by experience. Hierarchy is a universal way of structuring and of containing anxiety, but this can be abused at the expense of reality considerations and obstruct the free movement of affiliative open communication and information flow within a system, tending therefore to restrict this very freedom adversely. It is over matters of this sort that the social psychiatrist should be able to make pertinent administrative contributions.

Training Groups

What usually emerges from the administrative staff meetings is an increasing need for further training, for more specific focusing on particular aspects of the work, for instance conducting or selection. These training groups have a dual function and may range from a formal didactic setting, with lectures and seminars dealing with specific topics – for example, listening to tape-recordings of group sessions, watching video-tapes, or discussing a particular article or book, relevant to the work – to another extremely valuable dimension, usually known as T, or training, or sensitivity groups, where awareness to personal experiences, inter-personal relationships and emotional factors are taken into account. In fact, T-groups were first conceived by the social psychologists. Kurt Lewin, in the United States in the industrial field, and involved an emphasis on the experiencing and verbalizing of feelings. This was in 1946, shortly before his death in 1947, and it was his followers who first used the term sensitivity and later, in 1952, applied the name T-group. Gosling *et al.* in this country, at the Tavistock Institute of Human Relations, worked along similar lines and called their groups 'study groups', with the main emphasis on studying the group dynamics and tensions of the particular group in which the members are currently participating.

The crux of the matter is that, up to this point, groups have tended to have agenda, or occupations, or tasks, and the relational and emotional factors have been overlooked. With the introduction of awareness of these factors within the situation, a new dimension has emerged on a continuum between work at one end and psychotherapy at the other. The conductor has then to gauge in any given situation an optimal range depending on its actual membership and on the state of the group at any one moment, or at any one meeting; for example, the degree of skill, sophistication, training and experience of its members, and also their neurotic involvements and the climate of the environment or institution in which these meetings are taking place. For instance, there is no sense in, let us say, discussing a focal problem if the members are more concerned with a recent Regional Hospital Board circular recommending their dissolution! A common experience has been that unless the conductor is pretty clear about the direction of the group as a whole in relation to the total situation with other groups, the proceedings have a tendency to become involved with the personal problems of its individual members; in other words, with their own psychotherapy. This can be off-set by the conductor being alert to the tendency.

The conductor then needs to be quite clear in his own mind where the emphasis in any particular T-group is being placed, keeping in mind the dual nature of the situation which faces work or task on one side, and therapy on the other; he has to assess where, at any moment, to focus his attention, ranging somewhere on a continuum between psychotherapy, group therapy and group dynamics at one end, to learning, training, task or work at the other.

Seminars

Teaching of theory and techniques related to the day-to-day work is another important aspect. Seminars in both individual and group psychotherapy are essential in helping to increase skills.

Co-therapy, when two people share the responsibility of group leadership, is useful in training for group work. It has the advantages of offering mutual support, the opportunity of discussing the experience of the group, and, should one of the therapists leave, the group can continue with the other, possibly with the introduction of a new co-therapist later. Occasional difficulties may arise, where there are personal or theoretical differences between them, but these can usually be overcome by full and honest confrontation in the seminars. Alternatively being a participant observer whose role is non-interpretive is often easier to accept, and may be a more appropriate learning experience for the unskilled.

FIVE

Group Features, Group Theories and Therapeutic Principles

The dilemma of the individual confronting his group in dealing with his social context has always constituted a major problem throughout the history of mankind. Indeed it might well be said that psychological disturbances all bear some relationship to this conflict; for instance, Freud in his early writings assumed two sets of opposing psychic forces or drives which he spoke of as the sex instinct versus the moral instinct.

The American social psychologist, William Cooley, as long ago as 1902 described primary or face-to-face groups as 'the nursery of human nature', which included the play groups of children and the neighbourhood groups of adults. Primary groups have always more or less succeeded in functioning, but it is at the level of the larger secondary groups where communication is no longer face to face, that group contact becomes tenuous; it may indeed break down completely with the result that civilizations have come and gone as these secondary structures arise. When they collapse, the individuals involved suffer both psychologically and physically.

In small group therapy a small primary group setting is exploited in the sense of attempting to re-establish the contact between the individual and the group, which is sufficiently small on the one hand to enable the individual to express his innermost world personally, and sufficiently large to feel representative of a group or even of the community.

All groups may indeed be placed somewhere in a triangular area between psychology, group dynamics and work task or occupation, with group dynamics at the top, individual psychology on the left side of the bottom angle of the triangle, and work or task on the right *(Figure 5.1)*.

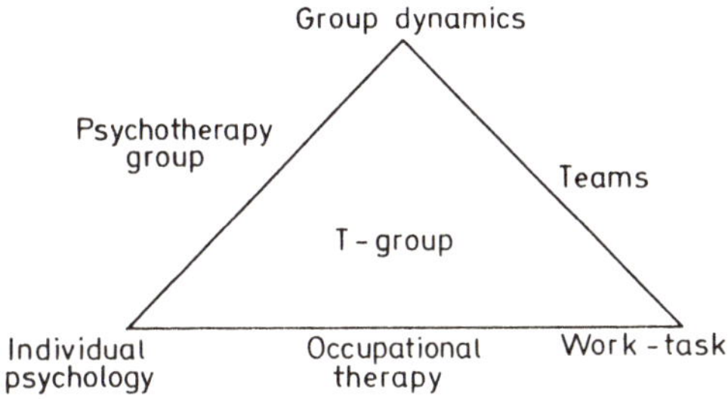

Figure 5.1

Freud made a statement concerning psychoanalysis to the effect that 'where Id was, there shall Ego be'. Group therapy would seem to have begun where Freud left off and perhaps it would be true to say of it that 'where super-ego was, there shall group be.'

GROUP FEATURES

Let us now turn to the specific features of groups which can be broadly categorized under three main headings: (*a*) activation; (*b*) communication; and (*c*) socialization.

Activation

What are the main characteristics of activation? As a crude example one might mention the way in which a crowd can activate itself into mob violence or panic. A well activated unit, such as a highly trained tank crew, can be activated to face almost any danger, which is described as having high morale. This activating power of the group situation has been found to be a powerful factor in remoulding and shaping individual opinions and, in many ways, is far more effective than the individual approach in persuading people to alter their attitudes and supplement learning processes generally. Other features of activation can be seen in such phenomena as supportiveness, 'togetherness' and enthusiasm. The group is a generating source of energy, which, given the opportunity of meeting, creates increasingly appropriate containing structures.

Communication

Communication is the second most striking feature of group processes and ranges from non-verbal messages such as bodily equivalents, gestures, postures and facial expressions, to highly evolved and sophisticated methods of exchange, such as conversation and free-floating discussion. It has been said that therapy lies at both ends of the communication scale, by which is meant that the essence of successful group psychotherapy resides in promoting a freely evolving network of communication.

Socialization

Out of these activities emerge certain patterns of relationship which, broadly speaking, could be categorized under the heading of socialization, involving the adoption of attitudes, roles, inter-personal relationships and personality which are both individually and socially valid. A group has been compared to a hall of mirrors where people become located in relationship to each other. They become aware of themselves in this relationship, and also in context to such matters as authority, leadership, the scapegoat, and group structuring of all kinds; it can become a training ground of enabling and corrective experiences or alternatively, if badly conducted, a constricting and inhibiting experience.

GROUP THEORIES

As we have already mentioned, all groups can theoretically be placed within a triangular framework somewhere between the three points of group dynamics, individual psychology and function, such as task occupation or work. On the whole, no group operates without showing some of the features of all three of these aspects. It is unlikely, therefore, that one will in fact be conducting a group on the lines of pure group dynamics. On the other hand, a group that functions as a work team is not likely to be primarily therapeutic. Equally a group which is individually psychoanalytically orientated can easily cease to be a group at all and therefore hardly deserves to be called group psychotherapeutic. The ingredients of a group-psychotherapeutic group are located on a continuum somewhere between individual psychotherapy at one end and group dynamics at the other with minimal emphasis on a group task as such. A social club, on the other hand, may place less emphasis on individual psychotherapy and can best be seen on a continuum between group dynamic and group task or occupation. Psychodrama tends to emphasize individual psychotherapy and drama as its major function.

The application of these ideas therapeutically brings us to the various schools or techniques seen in group psychotherapy and covers a wide range from a variety of disciplines including psychoanalysis, existential analysis, learning theory, to a range of 'system' approaches which have come to be known as 'structuralism', viz. Gestalt psychology, field theory, conflict theory, games, general systems, information and communication theory.

Psychoanalysis

Psychoanalysis is both a treatment and a theoretical system. It was evolved from the work of Sigmund Freud and is represented by many schools which have developed along somewhat different lines. As a treatment it is the most comprehensive form of individual psychotherapy there is and requires daily attendances over a period of four or five years. For this reason, it is only available to comparatively few people. On the other hand, as a theoretical system it has made a major contribution to the understanding of mental illness and other disciplines including anthropology and sociology. More specifically, it adds greatly to the understanding of group dynamics and many psychoanalytic concepts find their immediate relevance in group work. For example, the concept of the unconscious, of transference, projection, and the basic rule of the psychoanalytic method of free association finds its equivalent expression in the promotion of group association, that is the extended use of free floating discussion.

The three major approaches in psychoanalytically orientated group therapy are: Psychoanalysis *in* groups; psychoanalysis *of* groups; psychoanalysis *by* groups.

Psychoanalysis in groups was perhaps the earliest attempt to bring psychoanalysis and group therapy together and essentially might be described as psychoanalysis of the individual in a group setting, a technique which was first adopted by two psychoanalysts, Wender and Schilder, during the late 1930s in the USA. Later, during the 1940s, this technique was elaborated by Alexander Wolf and Schwartz, also in the States, who extended the technique to a fairly strictly psychoanalytic model of psychoanalysing groups.

However, *psychoanalysis of groups,* rather than in groups, which places an emphasis on the identity of the group as a whole, was primarily evolved by Bion at the Tavistock Clinic, and also by Ezriel and Sutherland. Bion described a group mentality which had three modes of behaviour based on three basic assumptions, namely: dependency, fight-flight, and pairing, which interfered with the successful working of group communication, which he described as a work group. Until these basic modes had worked themselves out or had responded to interpretation by the therapist, no really successful therapy, Bion believed, could take place. In this he was influenced greatly by the constructs of Melanie Klein, notably the paranoid and depressive positions and projective identification (see Glossary).

Ezriel, on the other hand, described 'the common group tension' and proceeded to analyse the individual's role in relationship to this common tension in terms of the 'here and now'. He employed a 'three tier' interpretative technique, involving the 'required relationship', the 'avoided relationship', and the 'calamitous relationship'. The Tavistock Clinic and the Institute of Human Relations base their group techniques, theories and studies on the works of these writers.

As distinct from these two approaches of psychoanalysis in groups, and of groups, Foulkes and the Institute of Group Analysis place the emphasis on *treatment by the group* itself. The conductor attempts to help the group to learn to function as a therapeutic agent. It is probably true to say that it was Foulkes who first conceived of group association as equivalent to free association and attributed interpretative meaning of one member's association to another as of primary therapeutic value with which he, the conductor, was concerned mainly as a catalyst with the psychoanalyst's attitude of receptivity, permissiveness and non-interference. His attitude, therefore, is psychoanalytic, but the method and technique are different.

Group Dynamics

From sociology, from such widely differing aspects of the behavioural sciences and anthropology and industrial psychology, emerged an intensive study not of large groups, but of small groups; for example the informal factory groups and street corner gangs. In 1939 Kurt Lewin, a Gestalt psychologist, first introduced the term 'group dynamics'. Borrowing from modern physics he described groups in terms of field theory in which the focus of attention was primarily not on the individual *per se,* but on their interaction and relatedness, and with the Gestalt approach he saw the group situation as a whole which consisted of something other and more than the sum of its parts. Be it said that the Gestaltists were influenced in their thinking by the phenomenology of Husserl, and earlier still by Marxist philosophy.

However, it took the impetus of World War II to bring group and psychodynamics together. The mass problems pertaining to modern warfare, involving matters of morale and selection procedure, needed more manoeuvrable and operationally applicable techniques which had a profound influence on psychiatry generally. This was brought about by the pressure of sheer expedience. Group psychotherapy and the therapeutic community for the first time came very much to the fore.

People like Bion, Rickman, Foulkes, Maxwell Jones and Main played a crucial role in the development of these approaches, whilst from the States and under somewhat different circumstances the culture pattern theorists and neo-Freudians, as they were called – most of whom were psychoanalysts originating from Europe – brought an increasing realization of the significance of social and cultural patterns; for example, such writers as Fromm, Erikson, Horney, Moreno, Slavson and, above all, Kurt Lewin.

Along somewhat different lines the Europeans, particularly Jaspers and the phenomenologists and the existentialists became involved with the philosophical dilemma of the individual in what appeared to be an increasingly alienating technological age.

Whatever their differences, the crux of the whole movement of group dynamics is that for the first time in history a serious scientific attempt was being made to relate the disciplines of natural science, psychology and sociology, with each other. The essential feature of group dynamics is the introduction of the social dimension into the very fabric of the technique of psychotherapy itself. From early days in sociology the formative influences of group pressure, involving personal and individual behaviour had become increasingly evident. For example, phenomena such as panic and mob violence was only manifest in relatively large groups and the controls and organization of large groups had to be far more rigidly enforced – as distinct from small groups. In other words, such factors as size, number and proximity, played a determining role. These were clear to such sociologists as Durkheim, Simmel and Weber. We have already mentioned that the social psychologist, Cooley, had described the small or primary group as the nursery of human nature, and 40 years later Kurt Lewin, the Sherrifs and others, had scientifically demonstrated the relationship between group membership and perception, between group climate and individual learning processes. For example, Lewin showed conclusively that democratically structured student groups learned more effectively than those which were conducted along either autocratic or *laissez faire* lines; he noted a tendency for scapegoatism to occur in authoritarian group settings. In fact, what we do in group therapy is an attempt to harness these forces for psychotherapeutic purposes. This then confronts the group conductor with something of a dilemma; on the one hand he has to interpret and analyse, and on the other he has to refrain from directing the group in favour of adopting a heuristic self-teaching attitude.

Communication and Information Theory

Shortly after World War II an engineer, Norbert Weiner, began writing about a strange circuit system in machines, which he called 'feedback', and which appeared to demonstrate goal-directed behaviour such as occurs with thermostats. This new development he called 'cybernetics' which literally means self-steering, and which covered not only the automatic control system of mechanical and electrical communication but has been extended to the nervous system, the brain, and to society. The significance of cybernetics for psychology and sociology has been enormous. Don Jackson gives as an example the man who kicks a pebble in which it is energy that is transferred. On the other hand, kicking a dog may result in a bite when it is not energy but information that is transferred. Conceiving the small discussion group as a self-regulating communicational system, which can possibly be harnessed for therapeutic purposes, is fundamental to the whole idea of group therapy. Equally, we must not overlook the possibility of such a system being anti-therapeutic if mis-used. Whilst the phenomenon of transference constitutes the cornerstone of the psychoanalytic situation, the total network of communication plays a similar role within group therapy, and has given rise to Foulkes' construct of the group matrix.

The judicious handling of the interplay between these elements – namely that of transference phenomena and communication in such a manner as to be deemed therapeutic – constitutes the basis of group psychotherapy.

Learning Theory

This is essentially a body of psychological theory which seeks to explain behaviour in terms of learned responses to the environment, in contrast to dynamic theory, such as psychoanalysis. It is an extension of the work of Pavlov, and provides the theoretical basis for behaviour therapy, in terms of deconditioning and relearning.

Since learning theory seeks to explain behaviour in terms of response to the environment and to the testing of reality, and since the group situation highlights mal-adaptive behaviour, group therapy inherently employs some of these principles to a greater extent than other forms of psychotherapy.

THERAPEUTIC PRINCIPLES

We have already looked at group features and theories and it became clear that there are many different ways in which group functioning can be viewed. However, within this complexity there are certain aspects which stand out as important areas for our consideration, particularly those which can be used for therapeutic purposes.

The headings we used were those of activation, communication and socialization. Let us return to these in greater detail in their therapeutic context.

Activation

In setting up a group, we create a situation which inevitably leads to interaction and participation. Our object is to promote a structure which will do this as effectively and as rapidly as possible. We therefore consider carefully all matters relating to selection, number, arrangements and early procedure in order to enable activation to occur as optimally as possible, and which we will examine in greater detail in the next chapter on 'Conducting a group'. Activation then leads on to communication.

Communication

We have already taken a brief look at the processes of communication, and the most valuable aspect in group therapy is to encourage the development of the free communicational network within the group. When a therapeutic group is first formed, communication tends to be hierarchical in structure; for example, the members tend to address the leader of the group and conversation is channelled mainly to or through the group conductor. If the group leader does not respond to being placed in this position by refraining deliberately from teaching, the group may elect their own leader with similar results, namely that communication tends to be centred on a new leader selected by themselves. In the course of time and with judicious handling of this phenomenon, communication becomes freer and less leader-centred. This change can be defined by the diagram *(Figure 5.2)* taken from Foulkes and Anthony's book, *Group Psychotherapy*.

Figure 5.2

The importance of this change in the patterns of communication is an indication of the growing confidence and sense of security within the group. It becomes less necessary constantly to test out the leader in order to discover what is and what is not permitted within the group.

Another pattern is that of pairing which is a feature described by Bion when two members talk to each other and the remainder appear to sit back and listen passively. This can be illustrated as shown in *Figure 5.3.* Pairing tends to split and disrupt the group and its meaning should be made manifest if the group is to grow and develop.

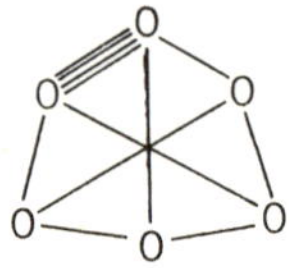

Figure 5.3

Silence itself may be considered as a means of communication and the understanding of silence within a group can lead to the enriching of the group experience. Silence can have a multitude of meanings, the context in which it occurs often being the indication of the underlying conflict. For example, silence may be the manner in which a sense of hopelessness and inadequacy is imparted to the leader, or the hostility and tension which is developing within the group is so intense that total inhibition is necessary to control what otherwise could become an explosive situation. On the other hand, it can be a positive response, indicating that generative processes are taking place. With increasing experience it becomes easier to manage group silences in a more constructive way, and it is often the inexperienced group leader who finds that frequent or prolonged silence is a feature of his group's life.

Foulkes has described certain characteristics that are quite specific to the group situation, e.g. sharing, exchange, chain and mirror reactions and others which are referred to elsewhere and cannot, for lack of space, be elaborated on here. However, there are two we should like to mention, notably:

Resonance

This term conceives the selectivity of unconscious communications within the group, so that other group members will 'resonate' to a particular theme that is presented by a participant. Thus, a particular topic or area of conflict is thrown into relief, giving it a greater clarity than might have occurred in individual treatment. This process of delineation of events of foreground against background, Foulkes has termed *location.*

Polarization

Complex group reactions become split into their component parts, and are expressed clearly at either end of the emotional spectrum. They become pure cultures, as it were, of the previously mixed reactions. There is a tendency to go to extremes, which again helps to clarify what is going on in the group. For example, ambivalence may be split into the poles of loving and hating, often expressed by two separate members adopting distinct attitudes.

Socialization

Emotional and mental disturbances manifest themselves essentially as disturbances in relationships. The promoting of meaningful participation in a social context can be seen as a characteristic feature of many successful therapeutic endeavours and might almost be regarded as synonymous with the psychotherapeutic aim itself. The event of the group then consists of a spiral development within a group structure, initiating a process of communication, out of which emerges the content or meaning which we have termed socialization. For the individual member the group situation may constantly be changing in significance and may range from the extremes of leader centred authoritarianism at one end to a group-orientated forum at the other, with intervening gradations of family equivalents.

We shall now turn to considering some of the important mechanisms which form an integral part of group therapy as well as being seen elsewhere in other psychotherapeutic settings, such as psychoanalysis.

Transference

By the term 'transference' we mean the spontaneous but unconscious emergence of feelings towards a person in the 'here and now', transferred from an earlier significant figure, for example, a parent from the past or 'there and then'. In psychoanalysis, which is a two-person, one-to-one, relationship, there develops the transference neurosis which in itself replaces the original symptoms or personality difficulties in the more understandable arena of the analytic relationship. In the group, on the other hand, the transference phenomenon becomes dispersed on to a broader front of multi-personal relationships between the members of the groups. On the whole in the early stages of the group's life, the transference tends to be centred on the leader, so that it is common experience that the majority of spontaneous feelings that emerge in the group are focused on him. For example, a member may experience fear of the conductor and adopt a passive, obsequious attitude as a way of defending against expressions of hostility from the conductor, thereby re-enacting the manner in which he attempted to handle the fear that he had of his father's rages in earlier years. In the later development of the group, overwhelming jealousy towards another member over having to share the conductor's attention might occur, thus repeating a sibling rivalry from the family past.

However, the group, as distinct from the psychoanalytic setting, displays a greater emphasis on the reality of relationships so that transference plays a less specific role. Indeed, we suggest that a different term might be appropriately employed referring to this aspect, namely 'transposition', which would imply a transposing of contexts, past, present or even of the fantasized future, to the group setting. This network of relationships can become highly emotive in a manner that has provoked some writers to see certain group responses in the light of more primitive sociological manifestations; for example, Freud's construct of 'The Primal Horde Leader'.

Splitting

By the term 'splitting' is meant the division of feelings into component parts. For example, apparent indifference may give way to powerful expressions of love and hate. The earliest experience of splitting is that of the infant in relationship to the breast or breasts. In the first few months of life one can imagine the infant relating to two different breasts, the good one that feeds and gratifies and the bad one that deprives and frustrates. The infant's feelings of loving and hating are split and it is only later that the infant becomes aware that it is one and the same breast that both feeds and frustrates. This realization of the loving and hating being directed to the one object gives rise to feelings of depression in place of the earlier ones of persecution. In psychoanalysis, splitting is predominantly seen in terms of one object, namely the analyst, when good and bad feelings tend to be experienced alternatively. In group analysis, these can and do occur concurrently towards both individual members and sub-groups. For example, a group member may consistently experience hostility and destructive feelings towards another whilst maintaining a friendly and helpful attitude towards a third person within the group. The clarification of these split emotions and how they become attached to different people is an important aspect of group work.

Projection

By the term 'projection' is meant the unconscious process by which certain feelings or ideas are disowned and attributed to other people or outside objects. For example, a man with strong homosexual tendencies may deny those in himself but accuse others of making homosexual advances towards him, i.e. the feelings are projected outwards. The group setting lends itself to the expression of highly complex projective manifestations similar to those seen in splitting, the elucidation of which constitutes very much part of the essential group work. For example, a silent, retiring member may accuse the others of being too demanding of the group leader's attention in an attempt to deny his own greedy impulses. A final extension of projection is the Kleinian construct of projective identification which has been emphasized by Bion, in which the denied feelings are pushed into others rather than merely on to them and the patient becomes attached to the people who now contain, as it were, parts of himself and without whom he may experience a feeling of loss, depletion and emptiness. The group conductor is often on the end of these projective identifications, and this experience can be of great value in helping him to empathize with the deeper, unconscious manifestations within the group; in other words, to regard the acceptance and acknowledgement of projective identifications, as a means of illuminating the therapist's counter-transference – that is, his own reactions to the group transference.

To quote an example, the conductor may develop an intense feeling of inadequacy, of inability to cope with the overwhelming demands of the group. His own experience of helplessness in this instance may well indicate that he is receiving the projection of identical feelings from the group, so that he can use this to interpret the unconscious processes that are present.

A major problem is highlighted by this mechanism, in the sense that it may prove difficult to be sure how far the counter-transference is a valid appropriate response to the transference manifestations within the group, or is it the expression of the personal neurotic conflict (or psychopathology) of the therapist? Clearly it is unhelpful for the conductor to interpret the group experience on the basis of his own unresolved hang-ups. This is one important reason why a prospective group therapist should obtain therapy – or at least the experience of a training (T) group – for himself.

SIX

How to Conduct a Small Psychotherapeutic Group

People tend to ask this question first – namely, how to conduct a group – but we have left this topic until last, having already considered the nature and processes generally of the group itself.

The small group is our basic model since it epitomises the essential meeting point between the individual and society. The fascination of the small group is that it allows the individual to retain his identity whilst also permitting him to relate and interact with others, these on-going processes, both individual and group, being concurrent and simultaneously observable. In this sense the small group can hardly be over-rated as a unique and potentially highly therapeutic setting.

The importance of the small group was largely recognized and promoted by clinical psychologists in the first place during the 1930s, and has since been extended to other fields including those of industry, education, criminology and sociology. Here we wish to focus on its original psychotherapeutic function. It was Freud who pointed out the dilemma of the individual in relationship to society, that where the individual cannot cope with society he tends to become neurotic; alternatively if society cannot cope with him he is regarded as criminal or psychopathic.

Group therapy received considerable impetus as a technique during World War II and was adopted in order to save time in the handling of large numbers of cases of neurosis, particularly those of battle-exhaustion, as it was then called. Although it was initiated as an expedient measure, it was soon discovered to have its own characteristic therapeutic potential. It was therefore, and has now become, a recognized form of psychotherapy and has made psychotherapy available to a far larger number and a wider range of patients than would otherwise have been possible. The valuable concepts and insight revealed by psychoanalysis for instance, could now be applied in a more general context.

We shall describe the principles of conducting in terms of how to start, how to proceed, and how to terminate a group.

HOW TO START

Let us take a practical example. Somebody wants to form and conduct a small psychotherapeutic group, already having had three referrals who might be suitable for each other, namely two men in their early thirties and a woman in her late twenties. Essentially they each have neurotic problems, are of reasonably good intelligence, are able to verbalize and are well motivated. Here then would seem to be a satisfactory nucleus with which to form a group. The conductor will now need to apply certain other principles of selection. These are primarily based on the personality as a whole and on the shared capacity of the members to make use of the group setting mutually rather than upon symptomatology and this he does partly from the documents, from discussion with colleagues or from referrals he himself has interviewed. He proposes to select a further four or five patients, making a total of seven or eight, with preferably an equal number of men and women, or a ratio of three to five, or even a greater difference if this is unavoidable, but one man or one woman on their own is inadvisable as the setting may then tend to provoke feelings of isolation or over-active Oedipal anxieties.

He will be inclined to select those patients who have a similar level of intelligence, of not more than a ten-year span in age between each other suffering basically from neurotic conflicts and all equally well motivated. On the whole, it is advisable to select patients of roughly the same level of psychological sophistication and treatment experience. These factors aim at the ideal but of course in reality it may not be possible to apply them rigorously and the scatter may have to be wider. For example, there may be an insufficient number of patients of the intended age group, in which case a younger or older patient of 19 or 43, for example, may have to be included, or alternatively a borderline patient or one who has emerged from a psychotic illness with reasonable capacity for insight. On the other hand, if it is proposed that the group be a closed one and likely to continue over an extended period a more careful selection may have to be maintained in order to do justice to the group's potential. It is usual for the therapist to have seen all the referrals initially at an individual interview for assessment, in which case once the acceptable number has been chosen the next step is to make the arrangements for the group's first meeting; this, if so desired, can be acknowledged as a preliminary or provisional introductory meeting.

The therapist should be clear in his own mind as to the possible time and place, frequency and duration of the group sessions, and whether to work alone, or with a co-therapist. The seating arrangements will already have been organized, usually in a circle around a small table. Most meetings are weekly and last an hour and a half. In the first session, he will have to discuss arrangements and early procedure, for instance he might encourage punctuality and regularity of attendance. He may also discuss the question of meetings outside the group, stating his view and advice to the effect that these contacts should be minimal and, if they do occur, should be brought up at the next session. Members might be encouraged also to leave messages if they are unable to attend for any reason, and if absence continues for a number of meetings the matter should certainly be scrutinized and the situation regularized. Holidays as far as possible, should be taken at the same time. Having discussed the practical arrangements the therapist should then cease to direct the group any further but should await spontaneous developments.

If the members start talking spontaneously, the therapist does not interfere, but rather prefers their contributions to his own, which will allow him the opportunity of a clearer view of the group development, and will also enable the members, as Foulkes pointed out, to take their own interventions more seriously. It is probably a good rule that so long as conversation is continued (group association, as it has been called), the therapist remains silent, which allows members to develop their own themes. If the conductor at an early stage indicates his own ideas, this may well influence further developments along the lines of his own pre-conceived thoughts which should, if possible, be avoided. It is probably a good idea to wait until either the conversation lapses into silence or alternatively becomes repetitive, in which case he should concern himself with surmising the possible reasons for this blocking in the flow of the free-floating discussion.

Alternatively, as happens not infrequently, when there is an embarrassed silence, the conductor can adopt one of two procedures. Either he attempts to understand the reasons for the silence and makes the appropriate interpretation or he encourages people more directly to start talking rather than leaving them to cope with tensions that may at this early stage be proving too much for them. When he interprets the meanings of a silence, it is as well that he tries to empathize with the atmosphere of the group as a whole; for example, it might be that the group waits passively for directives from the therapist which itself deserves comment. For instance, one might say 'I feel everybody is waiting for me to give a lead.'

It is very common for people to feel extremely anxious on the first occasion that the group meets and part of the work of the first session can be the voicing and understanding of these anxieties. For example, a person might be fearful over the possible revelation of matters of secrecy and privacy, and may be worried as to the degree of confidentiality. Another may fear exposing himself to the aggression of the other members in whom he may well feel a lack of trust.

The common themes that develop in the first session are getting to know each other, symptom-swapping, previous treatments, curiosity over the therapist and often concern the function of the group itself. In terms of getting to know each other, the therapist may have taken it upon himself to have introduced the members to each other. Alternatively he may leave this to the members themselves when one of the points of interest will be whether to use christian or surnames. Getting to know each other often alleviates initial tensions. Symptom-swapping may take the form of members inviting each other to disclose the reasons for their attending the group in the first place. Invariably there will be shared symptoms which again can alleviate members' anxieties in learning that they are not alone in their experiences, for example, fear of travelling or maybe shyness. Indeed this may promote a sense of group cohesion.

Previous or current treatments in the form of medication is a fairly common theme and this may well lead on to the comparing of experiences with different drugs, their curiosity as to the value of group treatment itself and the role that the conductor is likely to fulfill. Doubts of all sorts may be voiced or alternatively exaggerated expectations.

The importance of this first session is that it may well indicate for members the manner in which problems arising will be handled, either by the other members or by the therapist himself. Many therapists favour the development of a free exchange in an atmosphere that is reasonably secure and this, of itself, promotes general participation and avoids a situation of question/answer relationship with the therapist. Some of the embarrassment over the situation arises from the fact that this is unusual in the sense that here is a group which is neither led nor has a clearly defined occupation or goal.

In starting a group, the therapist himself may experience certain anxieties which can take the form of fear that the group will fail to develop and become established, or alternatively that several members will drop out. This, in fact, is quite common in the early stages of the group, particularly if the members for one reason or another have not been well matched. He may also entertain doubts as to his own abilities and experience as a therapist, and the success of the group generally.

The importance of these first meetings of a group cannot be overemphasized, since they tend to set the tone, pace and whole development of the group for the future. Handling of the early development is therefore crucial; for example it may be easier to ignore matters of absenteeism or unpunctuality, but this then creates an assumption that the group working as a whole, or the individual members' contributions are not important. Similarly whilst it may be necessary to give some answers to direct questions, if the conductor falls in too easily with this, the dependent passive aspects of the members may set the pattern and tend to constrict further developments.

HOW TO PROCEED

Like the individual, each group is unique and therefore different from every other. Accordingly, it is important for the therapist to maintain a flexible and open approach. Certain group traits should soon make themselves evident which are often quite characteristic for each particular group. At the same time groups seem to show a typical history into which some writers have chosen to read various interpretations, or analogies derived from the individual's development, for instance, the newborn baby and its totally dependent needs for the mother or maternal environment such as the womb or breast; similarly, the crises of weaning and early separation, mother/father/child relationships, sibling rivalry and sharing problems. Other writers, on the other hand, emphasize the social patternings that can be seen to emerge, such as leader-centred structuring, scapegoatism, and the emergence of groups of greater complexity and maturity such as group-centred groups, which undertake more seriously the solving of their own problems, sometimes described as work groups. Groups may be seen to fluctuate rapidly from one type of pattern to another. The procedure of a group of people working together tends to create the impression of a certain coherence of unity. A network of communication develops an entity of its own, which can be regarded on occasions as being highly therapeutic, since it offers an element of support for the anxious individual who is seeking security to solve his own isolating neurotic problems. Often during these early sessions there is a 'honeymoon period' of the group 'getting off the ground'; there is 'togetherness', and a sense of expectation and help, but the therapist should not be beguiled into seeing this as anything more than a phase, and probably an early one, in the group's development. People attend regularly, punctually, and appear optimistic; the therapist himself may be treated with special respect. This has sometimes been described as a dependent group. In due course, however, the likelihood is that the original problems that brought people into the group in the first place will emerge as equivalents within the group setting itself. Difficulties in relationships in communicating will re-appear in a new guise within the group context. Often the neurosis itself will meet with non-comprehension and tends to defy general understanding. On the other hand, the atmosphere fostered in the group should be such that the group, rather than operating as an efficient team, or 'good' group, is encouraged to adopt an attitude of enquiry and exploration. This distinguishes it from most other group situations, in providing what has been called an enabling or permissive atmosphere.

Let us assume that at this point the group has emerged as a working entity and people are talking more candidly without having to resort to those defensive maneouvres, which until then had been a prominent feature of their so-called psychopathology. Personal conflicts begin forming certain repetitive patterns in relationship to each other. In a way, one can feel the development in both vertical and horizontal perspectives. The individual expresses himself at deeper levels of his own personal experience and this he does simultaneously in relationship to the broader context of the group. In other words, this repeated re-statement of his problems becomes translated and re-moulded within the group network, a process which has been called locating or mapping. The true meaning of the symptom may therefore become disclosed in its significance in relationship to other people. For example, a demanding young man who has to date succeeded in tyrannising his own family by a sulky withdrawal and threats of suicide, encounters a group response very different from that of the family. Whereas his family may have repeatedly given in to the demands underlying his threats, the group rumbles this pattern of behaviour as an inappropriate way of achieving his ends.

There seems to be an interplay going on in the group between personal problems or symptoms, group topics, patterns in group structure and group culture, group atmosphere, tensions and tempo, static and dynamic and many other factors, all of which it is important for the therapist to be aware as far as possible. For instance, a dependent member may display the equivalent of this in the group by always sitting next to the therapist and refraining from making contributions or by minimal participation, tending if anything to slow the tempo of the group which becomes rather passive in nature, lacking in tension, to the extent of causing general apathy. This sort of culture may pass unnoticed by the group generally and if it continues too long may require intervention on the part of the therapist who thereby may release some valuable information which has become bound, as it were, in the particular patterning – a sort of hidden agenda as it has been called. As far as possible the therapist prefers the intervention by group members to that of his own but in the event of their apparent inability to do so he may have to intervene. In any case, he is more aware of these total group phenomena than the members themselves, who will be more deeply and spontaneously involved to an extent which renders them less aware of these factors. As for topics, the atmosphere in the group, it is hoped, will provide a sufficient sense of trust and security to make it possible to talk of anything they choose, whether trivial, seemingly irrelevant or profoundly intimate and personal. This sense of trust and security will allow for the expression of depressive feelings and is often associated with an atmosphere of dependency in the group. Alternatively, paranoid feelings will predominate in a group characterized by a hostile or frightened atmosphere, and may be adopted in order to avoid depressive feelings. Alternatively, another way in which a group deals with underlying depression may be by a manic denial into elation or flight into health. For example, a young student at the start of the group session immediately began to talk of an exciting weekend in which she had 'hitched' to a seaside resort, describing her complicated adventures in great detail, and in a pressurized manner. At the end of this account, the group was silent for a short time until another member reminded them of her concern about weekends which had so often led to dreariness and depression in the past. He suggested she was running away to avoid collapsing in despair.

To summarize the situation, Dorothy Stock Whitaker has put it that the development of a therapy group from its inception to its termination is characterized by the recurrence of basic themes under progressively expanding cultural conditions.

HOW TO TERMINATE

Some groups, particularly 'open groups' where there is a turnover of patients, may be interminable, that is to say the group itself goes on indefinitely but with a slowly changing membership. Other groups may have a fairly definite end point which has been stipulated from the beginning; for instance the conductor may know he is leaving his appointment at a definite time in the future and that rather than plan to pass the group on to another therapist, he decides to limit the duration to six months or a year. It is essential in this case that he keep drawing the group's attention to this termination date since this is only too easily overlooked. There may be no crucial reason why the group should not be passed on to another therapist, but if so, this will need to be discussed with the group members well in advance.

What are the factors that would determine one's decision to terminate a group?

(1) General improvement either symptomatically or in terms of personality and relationship problems; both the therapist and the members of the goup are satisfied that they have made good progress and no longer feel the need to continue. This would be the ideal outcome but more usually there are other factors as well which play a role in the termination of treatment, such as matters of personal expedience or different rates of improvement, with a consequent diminution in the membership.

(2) A decision reached by the therapist and/or the group members themselves that no further practicable progress can be made. Under these circumstances, there will probably be a sense of disappointment, but it may be advisable to terminate a group that is not progressing satisfactorily rather than to allow it to linger on indefinitely in the forlorn hope that a group mystique will bring about an eventual magical cure.

(3) Where termination is itself regarded as the important area of therapeutic endeavour – for example, situations where dependency plays a major role – the working through of separation anxiety with its attendant depression and sense of loss can be one of the most significant experiences provided by the group. In the individual setting, this principle has been emphasized by David Malan in his book, *A Study of Brief Psychotherapy,* in which one of the important conclusions is that it is necessary to deal with the problems of termination from the first session of treatment.

Criteria for termination can usefully be categorized under the headings of improvement as assessed by the patient himself, by the other members of the group, by outside impressions, e.g. work, social or family situation and by the therapist. The average duration of a group in which the turnover is relatively slow and the group as a stable structure would appear to be at least two years, if meeting once weekly. Duration of treatment, as for all forms of psychotherapy, depends both on the therapeutic needs of the patients and on the external pressures of availability of psychotherapeutic facilities. For instance, with brief individual pyschotherapy within a National Health Service setting, it may not be possible to offer more than once-a-week sessions, over a total period of 3–6 months. This short-term psychotherapy can be extremely valuable, even if there is a need for further treatment in a group thereafter, but for some patients, particularly those with severe or long-standing personality disorders, group therapy may be preferred from the outset, because of the greater flexibility of time that can be allowed.

The handling, or technique, of dealing with the process of termination of a group is vital. The conductor must be alive to the stresses inherent in the very nature of the experience. There may be intense depression and anxiety resulting from the threat of separation and abandonment, and this should be faced openly, no matter how painful, rather than for the group leader to collude with group defences against the pain, such as manic-denial. It is not uncommon, for example, for the fantasy to emerge in a group during the last few sessions of its life, in which they plan to go off for a 'manic feast' after the final meeting, the unconscious purpose being the provision of an oral experience, so intensely gratifying, that it will over-ride all feelings of frustration, loss and despair.

The process of resonance intensifies the depressive reaction of the group, sometimes to the extent in which a real sense of mourning emerges, and which can become almost unbearable in its strength. As with the process of mourning, resentment and anger may be felt and expressed towards the group or conductor. Again, it is far better for these feelings to come out, rather than be pushed away by denial, or over-idealization of the group experience. A factor indicating a good prognosis in individual psychotherapy, described by Malan, is when 'grief and anger at termination are important issues' (*A Study of Brief Psychotherapy*). It is likely that the same principle applies to group therapy. A recrudescence of symptoms, or problems in relationships, may occur in the closing phase of the group. Problems that were present at the beginning of treatment, and which may have diminished or vanished altogether during the group may emerge once again under the strain of termination, possibly a last-stand attempt to manipulate the group leader into abandoning the plan to stop, and instead to grant the group a new lease of life.

All these aspects must be respected, and as far as it is possible, worked through. In the same way that a baby has to be weaned from the breast, or that we must all face the inevitability of eventual death, so the group must accept the reality of termination.

It may be difficult to assess the results of group psychotherapy in the early period following the ending of treatment, because of the on-going emotional conflicts at this time. Often, it is not until much later, perhaps one year after the completion of treatment, that the full benefits are to be seen. Perhaps this has its parallel with the process of mourning, the conventional trappings of which are supposed to be maintained over a period of a year.

SEVEN

Therapeutic Community

Because of the vital role that group dynamics plays in the therapeutic community, the subject deserves a chapter to itself. The whole range of group work, from small to large, patient and staff, is essential to the running of the community if it is of itself to be of therapeutic value.

DEVELOPMENT

The term 'therapeutic community' was first used by Main in 1946, in an article entitled 'The hospital as a therapeutic institution'. His paper was one of several dealing with the experiences in psychiatric hospital practice during World War II. We have already given a short account of Northfield, so perhaps it is enough just to acknowledge once again the importance of that military hospital in the development of dynamic psychiatry.

If one were to pick out the person whose name is most associated with therapeutic community, it would unquestionably be Maxwell Jones, who more than anyone else devoted his energies to the development of such communities. In 1947 he started the Industrial Neurosis Unit at Belmont Hospital, later to be known as the Social Rehabilitation Unit, and yet still re-named the Henderson Hospital. Jones wrote his book *Social Psychiatry,* published in 1952, in which the experiences at this unit were related. In this book he defines the therapeutic community as follows:

> A therapeutic community is distinctive among other comparable treatment centres in the way the institution's total resources, both staff and patients, are self-consciously pooled in furthering treatment.

Dennis Martin was the superintendent at Claybury Hospital in the 1950s and he too wrote of his experiences in a book entitled *Adventure in Psychiatry,* in which he offered the following definition:

THERAPEUTIC COMMUNITY

> A therapeutic community is one in which a deliberate effort is made to use to the fullest possible extent, in a comprehensive treatment plan, the contributions of all staff and patients.

David Clark wrote his book entitled *Administrative Therapy* in 1964 dealing with the administrative aspects of the therapeutic community. He gives two definitions of administrative therapy, one of which is:

> The art of fulfilling the true doctor's role in a therapeutic community.

CHARACTERISTICS

What then are the special ingredients of a therapeutic community? Clearly the emphasis is on a greater equality between patients and staff, the doctors (amongst other staff) having to abandon their more traditional medical role. The 'Apostolic function' (as Balint terms it), the mantle of omnipotence, are anti-therapeutic, and although at times leaders of therapeutic communities have to assume a hierarchical position, if no alternative can be found, this should be a transient move to deal with whatever crisis situation precipitated its need. The importance of this abdication by staff of their hierarchical positions is that it allows or enables patients to find their own solution, albeit with the guidance that may be required. The concept of 'the group treating itself' is vital.

For this to happen, much work has to be undertaken by staff in examining their own roles, and one can hardly expect a democratic atmosphere amongst the patients if the 'pecking order' is maintained at a staff level. It is necessary to face the satirical comment of George Orwell, in his book *Animal Farm* – 'all animals are equal, but some are more equal than others'.

Freeing of the communicational network is another task that must be achieved, if the therapeutic community is to become a success. People (patient or staff member) must be able to express their feelings, needs, criticisms, even if illogical or irrational. The working through of problems in the various groups will determine the basic value or validity of the comments. Valvular communication – that is, where communication travels only one way (like blood in arteries or veins) – is a defect of many institutions and organizations, and causes ignorance, hostility and resentment.

David Clark has summarized the essential characteristics of therapeutic communities as follows:

(1) Freeing of communication.
(2) Analysis of all events.

(3) Provision of learning experiences.
(4) Flattening of authority pyramid.
(5) Role examination.
(6) Community meetings.

GROUP ORGANIZATION

One of the problems facing us is to determine the place of therapeutic community in the psychiatric units of the future. The difficulties of numbers and lack of selection do present themselves. The plans are for small psychiatric units of about 120 beds, sited in or near the general hospitals. Will it prove possible to run them on therapeutic community lines? Perhaps it will help describe the development at Halliwick, for this hospital has a total of 121 beds (plus 50 day hospital places).

Halliwick was opened in 1959, having been built as a general psychiatric unit. Provision was made for physical treatment, even an insulin unit, which was never used as such, but makes an excellent group room.

Originally there were two female wards and one male ward, with all consultants sharing the beds. In the male ward this led to considerable difficulty, the ward sister spending most of her time in attendance on the consultant rounds. Eventually things were re-organized, so that each of the three wards had both male and female patients, with only two consultants per ward. Mixed nursing (that is both male and female staff on each ward) occurred at the same time. Uniforms were abandoned, doctors discarded their white coats, and nurses wore their everyday clothes.

A wide spectrum of diagnostic categories are taken into the hospital, with both neurotic and psychotic cases. Geriatric patients are admitted only if they are considered treatable, with reasonably good prognosis in the short term. Adolescents are usually an active sub-group, and many students are referred. Treatment tends to be 'eclectic', that is to say, using the best methods for a particular patient, rather than sticking rigidly to one special approach, be it organic or psychotherapeutic. Drugs and ECT are used (sparingly on the whole), if considered appropriate. But essentially the whole hospital has been organized on group lines, and the group work that is undertaken is felt to be of the greatest value for patients.

The following is a summary of the group organization within the hospital.

Patient Groups

(1) Daily ward meetings: 9.30–10.30 a.m. All patients and staff on each of the wards attend; average attendance about 30 people.

(2) Small ward groups: Patients are divided into two smaller groups (about 12–15 in each), and each group meets three times a week: once with the consultant, once with the medical registrar, and once with the ward sister. This multiple, rotating group leadership works particularly well, offering the opportunity to examine 'split-transferences', for instance the difference in the content of the meeting between the group taken by the consultant and that by the ward sister (father–mother). Good communication between the three therapists is essential.

(3) 'Special groups': From time to time there is clearly a need for more intensive help for a sub-group within the hospital, not necessarily confined to one particular ward. For example, at one time there were about eight severely phobic patients in the hospital, so for about two months they met as a special group, with great success. At other times, the younger adolescents were formed into a group and whilst being a valuable experience, it also created a special problem!

(4) Crisis groups: Occasions arise when tension builds up in the unit as a whole, or in one of the wards, and the usual group facilities seem inadequate in handling the situation. When it begins to feel as if there will be an explosion, or if some piece of acting out has occurred, it may be necessary to convene a crisis group. For some reason, crisis groups always seem to be a great success, and almost always achieve their end. Perhaps it is the 'special' quality of them that creates an atmosphere of interest and excitement that may be lacking in the more routine groups of every day.

(5) Community meeting: Once a week the whole community meets; sometimes, when all patients and staff attend, as many as 150 people may be present. Although rather unwieldy, it is felt to be of great importance, particularly in symbolizing the 'togetherness' that may be lacking during the rest of the week. It also helps in dealing with tensions and rivalries that develop between wards, and the total atmosphere or emotional climate of the hospital can be gauged.

Staff Groups

(1) Following on patients' groups: It is most valuable for staff to meet, if only for a quarter of an hour, to discuss the preceding patient group. It is vital as a training procedure for younger staff, and also in

order to understand as fully as possible the implications of the events that occurred in the group.

(2) T-groups: Training or sensitivity groups for staff are necessary in order to allow them to explore their roles, and to deal with difficulties that arise in staff relationships. Often these groups become overtly therapeutic, when one staff member is in some trouble emotionally. On the whole, however, it is best not to use them as a treatment situation, and if staff need treatment as such, it is better for them to get it elsewhere. It is gratifying to experience the staff group 'working through' a specific problem; for example, the 'difficult patient' who makes demands of an intense and devouring nature on each and every staff member. The sudden realization of the patient's manipulative activities, together with a clearer understanding of its meaning, emerges to the general feeling of pleasure of achievement.

(3) Seminars: There are a number of seminars each week; for example a 'group leader's group', taken by one of the consultant psychotherapists as a means of supervising those members of staff who are running groups themselves, whether in-patient or out-patient. Another group meets to discuss individual psychotherapy, and in yet another a wider programme of topics, such as psychopathology.

In the out-patient department of the hospital, there are some twelve psychotherapy groups which meet regularly once a week and, interestingly, nine of these groups are being conducted by non-medical staff, of which three are nurses. Some are run by co-therapists, which has many advantages.

PROBLEMS OF THE THERAPEUTIC COMMUNITY

Zeitlyn (1967) in a paper in the *British Journal of Psychiatry* entitled 'Therapeutic community: fact or fantasy', raises some of the objections to the therapeutic community approach. He stresses the need for constant re-appraisal of the work, and warns against over-idealization of the method (which we would see as a manifestation of the dependent group). His main criticism seems to be that group meetings are time-consuming, and may be at the cost of thorough individual assessment of patients. Also, some patients may be rejected as unsuitable for this approach, particularly if they have poor verbal ability. The points raised in this paper must be considered seriously, and certainly it would be wise to heed his warnings. However, from our experience, it would seem that patients are more often poorly assessed in the milieu of the old type of mental hospital ward, when the ward doctor tries to see every patient for perhaps five minutes a week, rather than in the live setting of the therapeutic community. Often it is easier to make a valid assessment of a patient in a group situation than in a one-to-one relationship.

The concept of 'role-blurring', which is vital to the success of the therapeutic community approach, can also lead to difficulties. Given a highly experienced, insightful and mature ward sister, and a rather immature, recently qualified, and defensive junior doctor, the nurse may be very much better at understanding the group dynamics than the doctor. This can be very threatening to the doctor, whose very training is aimed at his becoming an authority.

Multiple group leadership, whilst being a valuable technique, may flounder on the rocks of poor communication. If the leaders who take the group in rotation fail to pass on information to each other, and to discuss the overall developments in the group, this can lead to the encouragement of manipulative acting out in the patients.

The place of large groups in the therapeutic community setting is unquestionable. We have already referred to David Clark's summary of the essential characteristics of therapeutic communities, and one of these is community meetings. It is in these large group meetings that everyone involved in the community, patient or staff, come together, with the unique opportunity this affords. But how are they to be run? Various problems of technique are posed, particularly in the structuring of the large groups. Should there be a chairman for the meetings, either a democratically-elected patient representative, or a staff member? Should there be an agenda, or is a free-floating discussion to be preferred? Is it best to concentrate on information exchange of a practical nature, or can the group be allowed to utilize the experience in a more psychotherapeutic way? The power of the large group is intense, and because of this it is essential that further research is undertaken in this area.

Administration is an integral part of the functioning of the therapeutic community. The effect of administrative bodies, for example hospital management committees and regional hospital boards, may be crucial to the very existence of the therapeutic community. The quality of interaction in these administrative committees may therefore be relevant to the attitudes of these bodies. Such committees tend to have a strong hierarchical organization. The chairman of a committee may have his own special high-backed chair, perhaps a gavel on the table in front of him. There is a strict, rigid agenda, which is adhered to because of the pressure of time, which makes it difficult for conflicts to be discussed in an open and free way. Communications are channelled 'through the chair'. This rigid structuring contrasts with the aims of therapeutic community organization of groups, which lie in the direction of removal of hierarchical controls, and freeing of communication.

Lastly, and perhaps the greatest problem of all, is the question of staff casualties in the therapeutic community. The strain of the emotional demands on individuals can be enormous, as it is very different from the experience of working in a traditional psychiatric hospital setting, with its well-defined role preservation between staff and patients. In such a traditional setting, it is easy for a doctor or nurse to deal with a difficult and manipulative patient by clinging to their authoritarian position, and utilizing the power that is invested in their status. It is much more threatening to have to confront the same conflict in the setting of equality of status that is present in a therapeutic community. Members of staff have to face themselves more honestly, and this invariably spotlights their areas of weakness and vulnerability. It is commonplace for individuals to become more aware of their own psychopathology, and this experience may well determine the need for therapy for themselves. Of course this may be to the good, in the sense that, ideally, every person who works in a setting that utilizes dynamic concepts should have some psychotherapy, in order to modify any pre-existing emotional conflicts or blocks; but without this help occasionally the pressures within the work situation can lead to a complete breakdown, or even a suicidal attempt. It is vital that colleagues should be alive to the difficulties that can arise, so that individuals can seek help and advice openly, rather than to struggle on alone, to the point of desperation.

For many, the experience of working in a therapeutic community can lead to personal growth and enrichment, in exactly the same way that occurs with patients.

Post-script

A member of staff in a senior position within a so-called therapeutic community was confronted in an administrative meeting, because of the lack of full discussion, over a decision taken hierarchically. He defended himself by saying 'I can't listen to every Tom, Dick and Harry'. The essence of a truly therapeutic community is precisely that 'Tom, Dick *and* Harry' all have an absolute right to be heard.

REFERENCES

Clark, D. H. (1964). *Administrative Therapy.* London: Tavistock Publications.

Jones, M. (1952). *Social Psychiatry.* London: Tavistock Publications.

Main, T. F. (1946). 'The hospital as a therapeutic institution.' *Bull. Menninger Clin.*, **10**, 66.

Martin, D. V. (1962). *Adventure in Psychiatry.* Cassirer.

Zeitlyn. B. B. (1967). 'The therapeutic community – fact or fantasy?' *Br. J. Psychiat.*, **113**, 503.

EIGHT

The Future

The community approach has come to stay, but which shall it be: therapeutic community or community therapy? If the present trend is anything to go by, it will certainly be the latter; with the whole change of emphasis from treatment in hospital towards treating people out of hospital where hospitalization is seen merely as an undesirable incident, it is envisaged that the main efforts in dynamic therapy will be undertaken in the out-patient department or in the community centre. Future developments and the provision of group treatment will be concentrated outside the wards of general district hospital psychiatric units. In any case, psychiatry as such may well become the province of the well-trained general physician, involving entirely physical methods of treatment with a consequence that psychiatrists will have voted themselves out of court, and the only distinguishing feature of the psychiatrist will be his non-medical skill in psychotherapeutic expertise. In a recent publication (*British Journal of Psychiatry* 1970, Vol. 116, pages 51–55, concerning the availability of psychotherapeutic services in Camberwell), Prof. Wing indicated that 'four times the number of patients might have been referred for specialised psychotherapy than actually received treatment' and this in spite of Camberwell being relatively well provided with psychotherapeutic facilities. Indeed the large number of patients referred to private practice for psychotherapy indicates the inadequacy of existing facilities within the National Health Service. We do not wish to enter here a discussion of the relative merits of individual versus group psychotherapy, but it is impossible to provide comprehensive facilities by using individual psychotherapeutic methods alone.

FACILITIES

We look forward to the time when the provision of group facilities will involve a broad spectrum of groups including day centres, hostel accommodation, social clubs and a wide range of small groups including for example, adolescent, marital, conjoint family, general well-selected psychotherapy groups representing all ages and educational backgrounds and conducted by therapists who have had basic training in group techniques, and have opportunities for their own on-going supervision and seminars. It is hoped these arrangements will become adequate for the needs throughout the whole country and not just confined to specially selected areas. In group psychotherapy a relatively large waiting list has the merit that judicious selection procedure in groups plays a crucial role when high specificity in selection is the aim, and a total spectrum of groups fitted to suit the specific demands in any particular area, for example, larger groups, such as social club facilities, may be more appropriate in some districts as distinct from others.

ADMINISTRATIVE CONSIDERATIONS

A more systematic and detailed grasp of organization and method is imperative (*a*) in relationship to local government administration – for example, the relationship between the hospital and the hospital management committee, the regional hospital board, and the Ministry of Health, as these essentially involve group phenomena and provide important themes for study; (*b*) in relationship to a closer scrutiny of the network of interaction and relationships, group dynamics and psychodynamics, in the population of the larger hospital units which often present problems that are clearly of ecological origin demanding group expertise; (*c*) in relationship to training facilities, a recent ministerial pamphlet suggested ways in which new developments in psychiatry should be followed up rather than dropped as they so frequently are when the originator leaves the hospital or retires. We have already described the development of training facilities in a therapeutic community which involves setting aside time for staff meetings and seminars. The value of these meetings can only too easily be under-estimated and their effect in promoting and containing stable yet dynamic flexible treatment settings can play an enormously valuable role. However, these networks are not created to order but require considerable time, interest and enthusiasm in which to develop, often necessitating a period of several years to emerge. Unfortunately, they can only too easily be broken up and destroyed with the injudicious transfer of staff, or by sudden changes in policy, or by neglect, indifference, or outside interference from administrative sources without prior consultation. This would underline the need for everyone connected in the development of such a project to develop and maintain a sense of purpose, even identity. This again demands time. At Halliwick Hospital at the present time for instance, out of a total of twelve out-patient groups, seven are being conducted by non-medical staff; nurses, PSWs, occupational therapists; the need is for this trend to emerge and grow since these members of the staff often being both mature and experienced represent an untapped source of therapeutic resources.

DEVELOPMENTS IN TECHNIQUE

In this book, we have attempted to describe group techniques that are currently regarded as acceptable, and might almost be said to be orthodox. However, the group situation involves a wide variety of features, any of which can be manipulated, emphasized, or extended, so as to constitute the basis for certain new approaches. Today there are many new schools of group therapy, utilizing special techniques designed to highlight those areas of group experience felt by many to have been neglected in the past. These variations include the introduction of changes in such matters as size of group (for example, the large group of up to 60 people), time (the 24–48 hour marathon groups), action techniques (for example, Gestalt-games, touching and awareness–expansion exercises). The concept of theme-centred, time-limited groups is clearly of expedient value, although perhaps somewhat restrictive in scope.

There is now a great deal of research being undertaken in all these, and many other areas, both in the United States and in this country. It would be beyond the scope of this short introduction to attempt to cover the whole field of these new developments, but perhaps we could mention just a few, which seem to us to be of particular interest.

Combined Groups

These are small groups in which all the members are also regularly seen individually by the group therapist. They seem to be of particular value for patients who have suffered from deprivation in childhood, and who are therefore encountering difficulties in trusting and becoming fully involved in the group situation. Borderline personality disorders also appear to do best with a combined approach, owing to the narcissistic damage they have experienced in the past. It seems that they must have the individual and personal contact, to enable them to utilize the group setting.

Marital Groups

These consist of three or four couples together with a therapist or two co-therapists. The value of this situation is that the in-built transference problems which are disturbing the marriage are made evident against the background of the group. One spouse can confront another's in a way of which they would be incapable with their own partner. The social dimension is introduced into the hot-house atmosphere of the marital relationship, so that the group setting for the resolution of marital conflicts is not merely an expedient measure. Indeed the potential demand for marital therapy that exists in psychiatric practice is very high, and the group approach may be the only possible solution to the problem.

Family Therapy

The shift of emphasis in recent years from the pre-occupation with the individual's neurosis to that of the deeper study and understanding of the family network, marks a significant advance in our whole conceptual approach to psychotherapy. We turn from the isolated individual system to the total family constellation, with the result that focal areas of maximal disturbance can be located with greater clarity. Families can be interviewed as one unit, or several families may be included in a larger group, where again it becomes possible to confront each other's intolerable conflicts and perhaps thereby negotiate more appropriate and fulfilling inter-relationships.

Large Groups

Social systems can be broken down into primary structures, which are face to face, and which can be subdivided into small groups varying from 3 to 20 people, and large groups from 20 to, let us say, 200. Secondary structures (those which are not face to face) are more tenuously related and include organizations of multiple group structures such as communities and the global groups of societies, nations, and race, and are constantly breaking down owing to hold-ups in communication and information flow.

To date attention has been focused in psychotherapy on the small group but recently we have begun to look at the potentials of large groups *per se* – of groups of, let us say, between 25 and 100 members, not as peripheral phenomena or adjuncts to other procedures, e.g. social clubs, board meetings, therapeutic communities, but primarily and in their own right and as stringently as the small group or psychoanalytic setting, with closed regular meetings of 1½ hours' duration over a period of a year or more.

This is not such a surprising suggestion since the notion that neurosis is a response to a maladjusted society is not a recent one (Cody Marsh, 1909; Trotter, 1916). Marsh's credo was 'By the crowd they have been broken, by the crowd shall they be healed'. Panic, for instance, is a large group phenomenon and is seen as a phobic condition when manifested within the individual; psychotic anxiety too, such as persecutory fear, readily becomes manifest in large groups – all of which suggests a possible breakthrough in the treatment of such conditions, as well as an approach to the manifold problems that the secondary group structures present, for example racialism. The large group for instance shows more purely group dynamic as distinct from psychoanalytic features than does the small group.

It is quite clear that an enormous pool of information lies vested in the large group, that it could become a highly sensitive instrument whose potentials are at present only very dimly envisaged. The adoption of large group psychotherapy would seem therefore to be a self-evident procedure. It presents a situation in which we are dealing with 'transpositional' contexts involving past, current and even future situations set up within the individual, for example problems of expatriation which are more in the nature of present on-going let us say 'horizontal' environmental phenomena – splitting, displacing, projecting – than such 'vertical' phenomena as transference. The problems for the large group are antithetically distinct from those of small groups and go beyond psychoanalytic and group-analytic constructs. For the small group and for psychoanalysis the problem lies in experiencing spontaneous feeling whilst for the large group it is thought-process that is in quandary. Communication and organization are the group's equivalent to consciousness – indeed the word 'consciousness' itself means a 'knowing something with other people'. The dilemma for the large group is its mindlessness which is compensated for by the development of certain techniques such as language. This the individual can make use of, rather in the manner that Oedipus answered the riddle of the Sphinx. He can think his way through the dilemma with the help of language, even though language is not itself a thought process.

Human beings, having progressed through various styles of thinking – pagan, religious, philosophical, scientific, psychological – are now on the brink of sociological awareness, of increasing socially-based insights – one might almost say 'outsight' as distinct from personal insight, of socio-politico-economic insights which so far seem to have remained outside the orbit of psychotherapy. Nevertheless, these social contexts, as every social worker knows, do intrude constantly and rudely. The precarious careers of therapeutic communities (Forrest House, Paddington Day, Halliwick Hospital) are in fact manifestations not so much of these systems themselves but of the large secondary group structures outside, within which they are attempting to function. Until we scrutinize more carefully these large group phenomena of, let us say, community therapy as distinct from the therapeutic community, these threatening situations will continue to recur. It seems we are trying to play ludo on a chess board.

Encounter Groups

Encounter groups go by many names, such as sensitivity training, confrontation, human awareness, and personal growth. Perhaps the most significant deviation is that of bodily contact or touch. The direct encouragement to express emotion without restraint is again typical, and goes against the old principle of verbalization above all else. In the United States, Esalen has become an important centre for promoting this approach, and in this country we are beginning to evaluate, in a more modest way, the possibilities for its application. For example, at Halliwick the art therapist at one time was running encounter groups, and many patients expressed their enthusiasm for the liberating effect of this experience. We regard it still as an experimental procedure, but certainly one which demands further careful assessment.

Marathon Groups

These are developed initially by George Bach, and essentially run continuously for 24–48 hours at a time, with no organized break for sleep. Meals are served in the room without disrupting the group proceedings. The emphasis is on self-disclosure, and intensive interpersonal confrontation. The fatigue resulting from lack of sleep contributes to the abandonment of social facades with increased truthfulness in self-revelation.

Self-understanding Workshops

This is an approach in mental health education in the United States, in which up to 60 people meet for two-hourly sessions, once weekly, over a period of several weeks. The workshops owe much to Carl Rogers' views on self-discovered learning in therapy and education, and self-confrontation. In this country, Mrs. Jane Abercrombie has applied analogous techniques as part of the education programme for medical and architectural students.

CONCLUSIONS

It is becoming increasingly evident that waves of neurotic – not to say psychotic – disturbances are making themselves manifest in our society today, particularly amongst the younger members; and the community facilities for coping with such massive problems as the drug scene are proving inadequate. We seem to be at the crossroads already mentioned, namely that of the therapeutic community versus community therapy. The former offers a critical mutative confrontation based on an intensive dynamic matrix involving all the staff and patients in a hospital setting. By its very nature there has to be a centre in which people come together, and hitherto this centre has been the hospital or ward. Time is a vital ingredient to the processes involved and it is our experience that six months is a minimal period for such processes to emerge, be contained and to some extent resolved. With the new concepts of continuity of care, which is the essence of community therapy, it will have to be faced that it is unlikely that patients will be able to remain in hospital this length of time, since the new estimates of the need for psychiatric beds as distinct from case assessment would entail a prohibitively rapid turnover. The recent recommendation has been made of 0.5 beds per thousand population, as compared with 3.4 beds per thousand five years ago. In many ways this is regrettable because again it has been our experience that the so-called therapeutic community, if allowed the opportunity to develop, offers a unique and powerful containing setting imposing confrontations that are evaded by other techniques. This is made doubly unfortunate since it also focuses upon, and gives opportunity to observe and gain, the deepest understanding of the processes of both groups and psychodynamic techniques. Should the future proposals be realized these skills will have to be transferred from the in-patient situation to the out-patient department and to the day-hospitals and community care, with an inevitable dilution and dispersion in therapeutic endeavour for both staff and patients. This will have to be the price paid in the interests of continuity of care. The challenge now will be how far these principles of the therapeutic community have been lost to posterity and how far they can be preserved and re-applied in these new settings. It may well be that the day hospital will become the focal point of therapeutic leverage.

To conclude, if the last two decades are anything to go by, changes for the future will continue to appear fast and furiously, necessitating a reconsideration and complete re-assessment of the entire situation from time to time. Perhaps, for instance, the provision for individual psychotherapy will have to be dramatically expanded, but it is our opinion that the basis for dynamic psychiatry within the National Health Service will remain that of the group psychotherapeutic approach. With further application and research, group techniques will continue to improve and it is our conviction that group therapy offers us a therapeutic tool of considerable potential and versatility.

Glossary

Acting out – A method of expression, usually non-verbal which replaces thought by action, and should be regarded as a form of communication. An infantile conflict situation may be re-enacted time and again as a repetition compulsion.

Adlerian – An approach developed by Alfred Adler (1870–1937), an early disciple of Freud who founded his own movement of individual psychology in 1911 with emphasis on the struggle for power, and social factors. Some of the earliest groups in the 1930s were called Adlerian groups.

Affiliative – A term sometimes used in connection with communication – referring to peer level as distinct from hierarchical interaction (see Hierarchical).

Anthropology – The scientific study of man, his origins, development, and place in social organizations.

Basic Assumptions – A term coined by Bion to the effect that at any given time the pattern of group behaviour is concerned chiefly with the emotional problems of dependency, fight–flight, or pairing. The basic assumption group constitutes the often unrecognized behavioural background to all groups as distinct from the work group. It appears to make the implicit assumption that the group must be preserved at all costs (see Work group).

Behaviour – In its most general sense this denotes the change, movement or response of any entity or system in relation to its environment or situation.

Borderline – A descriptive term referring to the mental state on the boundary between neurosis and psychosis; nowadays it tends to be used as a diagnostic category.

Chain Reaction – Group associations consisting of linked individual contributions occurring within the group, which is equivalent to 'free association' of psychoanalysis.

Closed Group – See Open Group.

Common Group Tension – An effect of the pressure of *underlying* shared unconscious fantasies of the members in a group which influences the course of the group associations; a term introduced by Henry Ezriel.

Communication – Every event occurring within the group that can be noticed, whether verbal or non-verbal, conscious or unconscious. When communication proceeds in one direction only it is described as valvular.

Co-therapy – Two people share the responsibility of group leadership, with the advantages of mutual support and the possibilities for discussion of the group experience. A valuable training procedure.

Counter-transference – The emotional responses of the therapist to his patient or group, or to their transferences to him. It may be a valid and appropriate response, but alternatively it may be the expression of the therapist's own unresolved conflicts.

Cybernetics – A term originally applied in engineering and introduced by Robert Wiener during the 1940s, referring to the study of automatic message control either in machines, or brain and nervous system. Communication and information theory use many cybernetic concepts such as feedback (see Feedback).

Depressive Position – A Kleinian term referring to 'whole object' relationships when the infant recognizes the possibility of total loss of the mother, with the attendant feelings of pain and guilt, resulting from the direction of destructive feelings to the loved object.

Dialogue – A conversation between two or more persons. The ancients taught that after mathematics we need to learn dialogue or discourse – 'the supreme science' as Plato called it. Monologue refers to soliloquy, and dualogue to a dialogue between two people.

Didactic – Literally, intended to teach; in groups implying a formalized leader-centred teaching situation as distinct from the group association technique which relies on the group learning from its own experience.

Double Bind – A term referring to incompatible contradictory emotional demands, made typically by the mother on the child and from which there is no escape, other than withdrawal into a psychotic state. It was originally introduced by Bateson in 1956 to describe a childhood experience which might lead to the later development of schizophrenia.

Dynamic – A loose term describing an approach both to psychology and sociology, essentially involving change and interaction in contrast to static descriptive approaches. Group dynamics was a term introduced by Kurt Lewin in 1939.

Ego – Freud originally employed this term to refer to the experiential self or 'I', but later used it objectively to describe that part of the mental structure which is organized and rational, as distinct from the id (the instincts or passions), and the super-ego (conscience) (see Id and Super-ego).

Existential – A philosophical term now employed in psychiatry giving priority to total subjective experience or 'being', as distinct from underlying forces or causal explanations.

Feedback – The information returned by a response to a communication. A term borrowed from cybernetic theory and now widely used in psycho-social situations such as therapeutic groups.

Freudian – A term descriptive of the psychoanalytic approach developed initially by Sigmund Freud (1856–1939); it is today widely applied to other fields including group psychotherapy (see Psychoanalysis).

Gestalt Psychology – A school of psychology that believed it necessary to analyse the whole, rather than just its parts. Kurt Lewin was an important Gestaltist who applied himself to groups.

Group – A number of individuals, three or more, connected for some purpose or by some circumstance.

Group Content – Consists of the ideas, feelings and attitudes which emerge through the group processes.

Group Matrix – A term applied to the total communicational network within the group, equivalent to the term 'mind' as applied to the individual introduced by S. H. Foulkes.

Group Process – The dynamic interaction and communication occurring within the group structure.

Group Psychotherapy – Any form of psychotherapy involving three or more patients in the treatment situation.

Group-analytic Psychotherapy – A form of group psychotherapy in which group dynamic and psychoanalytic concepts are applied.

Group Structure – The physical arrangements of the group; in small groups usually seven or eight members, with the conductor, seated together in a circle.

Hierarchical – Descriptive of an organization involving levels of ascending authority and power; it is a term often used in relation to hospital structures and systems of communication (see Affiliative).

Id – The unorganized part of the mental apparatus generating the instincts and passions, the source of all drives; a construct evolved by Freud.

Insight – Self-awareness or self-knowledge; the explanation of one's own and others' mental processes.

Interpretation – A statement offering an understanding of meaning rather than an explanation of cause; a valuable technique in psychotherapy which aims at insight.

Jungian – Descriptive of the school of Carl Gustav Jung (1875–1961), who was for a time closely associated with Freud in the early days of psychoanalysis, but later separated and formed his own school of analytical psychology. Religion, myth, archetypes, collective and racial unconscious are concepts which enter his formulations. Jung himself was never involved with group psychotherapy but, like other psychoanalysts, many of his followers have made significant contributions to group theory and practice.

Kleinian – Melanie Klein (1882–1960), a psychoanalyst who introduced influential theories concerning the psychic development during the first year of life (see Paranoid, Schizoid and Depressive positions, and Projective identification). Bion and the Tavistock Clinic workers have incorporated Kleinian concepts into their understanding of groups, with a certain emphasis on psychotic mechanisms.

Leader-centred Groups – Newly formed groups tend to be leader-centred, when communication is directed towards the therapist. In group psychotherapy, the therapist, unlike leaders in most other groups, refrains from perpetuating this role in order to promote the contributions of the other members.

Learning Theory – This is essentially a body of psychological theory which seeks to explain behaviour in terms of learned responses to the environment, in contrast to dynamic theory such as psychoanalysis. It is an extension of the work of Pavlov and provides the theoretical basis for behaviour therapy, in terms of deconditioning and re-learning.

Mirror Reaction – Foulkes has compared the group situation to a 'hall of mirrors' where an individual is confronted with various aspects of his social, psychological or body image.

Oedipus Complex – A stage in psychological development in which a child experiences the conflict of exclusively loving one parent (usually of opposite gender), and of hating and wishing to annihilate the other. This was first described by Freud in 1900 based on the ancient Greek play, *Oedipus Rex,* in which Oedipus unknowingly killed his father and married his own mother. In the group constellation, Oedipal conflicts are readily manifested in the members seeing initially the group setting in terms of a family and only later in terms of a social microcosm.

Open Group – This is a group in which the membership come and go fairly freely. This is in contrast to the closed group in which the original group meets for a specified course without either members leaving or new members being introduced. This is a surprisingly uncommon event and there is a tendency for groups to become slow-open, in which there is a slow turn-over in membership.

Paranoid–Schizoid Position – A Kleinian term describing the earliest phase of infant development during the first three months of life in which there is a relationship to 'part objects' (breast, penis), with splitting and projective mechanisms predominating.

Polarization – A group-specific mechanism in which complex emotional experiences become split into their component parts, thus to be seen more clearly at the opposite ends of the emotional spectrum (or poles). A term introduced by S. H. Foulkes.

Primary Group – A term coined by Cooley in 1902 who specified in primary groups as those with face-to-face association, of relative permanence, of relative intimacy, and a small number of persons involved; for example, the family, the neighbourhood. The psychotherapy group is of course a primary group. Secondary groups are those in which these features are lacking.

Projective Identification – A Kleinian term descriptive of the psychological mechanism in which parts of the self are unconsciously projected into, rather than onto, an object or person, with the implication both of depletion and possessiveness, when the object takes over the characteristics of the projected parts.

Psychoanalysis – A form of treatment of the neuroses developed by Freud in the 1890s and elaborated by subsequent workers. It is the most extensive and intensive form of psychotherapy there is and classically the patient attends daily over a period of four or more years. It involves free association, interpretation and transference. Other than in treatment, it has the widest implications for various disciplines, theoretical and philosophical.

Psychodrama – A form of group therapy involving the dramatic staging of symptoms or problems by the patient and others – fellow patients or members of the therapeutic team. It is a technique devised by Moreno during the 1920s.

Psychoneurosis – A group of psychological disorders of varied symptomatology (anxiety, hysterical conversion, obsessional rumination), resulting from psychic conflict – essentially between the instincts (Id), and the rest of the personality (Ego and Super-ego), and/or Society. Reality testing is relatively normal.

Psychopathology – A term describing abnormal functioning of the mind, used loosely to be synonymous with 'hang-ups'.

Psychosis – A group of psychological disorders in which reality testing is disturbed. Schizophrenia and manic depressive psychosis consitute the two main categories of the functional psychoses.

Psychotherapy – A form of treatment essentially involving communication and interaction. Verbalization, insight and sensitivity to emotional relationships are characteristic features. Individual psychotherapy is a two-person relationship – whilst group psychotherapy involves three or more persons.

Repression – The psychological process by which unacceptable impulses or ideas are rendered unconscious. In the individual the repressed ideas may be translated and expressed as symptoms. In the group, cultural factors play a dynamic role in determining what is or is not acceptable and in moulding the nature of repression.

Resonance – A group-specific mechanism in which emotional responses from other members of the group resonate to the theme introduced by another, thus intensifying its quality. A term introduced by S. H. Foulkes.

Role Playing – The function played by an individual in a group – which may be primarily determined by the individual's attitudes, personality and previous roles, which he brings to the group; alternatively, it may be the expression of the demands of the group as a whole; more usually there are collusive elements in both individual and group, e.g. the group may need a scapegoat, but also the individual may connive masochistically.

Scapegoating – The process by which a recipient (willing or unwilling) accepts the projections of others in the group. Sometimes there is an urgent need in the group to find a sacrificial victim to be punished, thereby avoiding more generalized violence, which might otherwise destroy the whole group.

Schizoid Position – A term introduced by Fairbain, which he saw as primary. Separation anxiety, dependency, and splitting play basic roles. Withdrawal, indifference, emptiness are characteristics as distinct from the anger of the depressive position of Klein.

Small Group – This is a recent concept for both psychology and sociology and constitutes the essence of group psychotherapy; it represents a crucial bridging between these two disciplines.

Sociology – This scientific study of human society, its origins and development.

Sub-group – Splinter group, sub-culture and sub-group are all terms for the splitting up of the group into smaller sections, which may lead to fragmentation or alternatively to consolidation for further development.

Super-ego – That part of the mental apparatus concerned with morality and self-criticism, partly conscious, partly unconscious. Loosely 'conscience'.

T-groups – Stands for training groups in which awareness and verbalization of relationships and emotions are regarded as essential parts of the learning process in relationship to the task; otherwise known as sensitivity or study groups and not to be confused with therapeutic or transference groups; first recognized by Kurt Lewin in 1947 and introduced into education in the United States of America in 1952.

Therapeutic Community – A term introduced by Main (*The Hospital as a Therapeutic Institution* – 1946), and developed by Maxwell Jones, who described it as 'distinctive among other comparable treatment centres in the way the institution's total resources, of both staff and patients, are self-consciously pooled in furthering treatment (*Social Psychiatry,* 1952). Martin defines it as 'one in which a deliberate effort is made to use to the fullest possible extent in a comprehensive treatment plan, the contributions of all staff and patients' (*Adventure in Psychiatry,* 1962). This is in contradistinction to community therapy which is outside the hospital setting and within the community itself.

Transference – A psychoanalytic term for the process by which a patient displaces onto the therapist feelings and ideas which derive from previous figures in his life. In groups, transferences may developmental rather than magical concepts. The work, as distinct from the emotional component of the group (see Basic assumptions), is geared to a task, but one never occurs without the other.

Transposition – A term introduced by de Mare to imply the transposing of experiential contexts to the group setting, as distinct from the more traditional manifestations of transference.

Work Group – A term coined by Bion descriptive of the mental activity in a group, similar to the secondary process of the ego, namely rationality, purposiveness, organization, reality testing, depending on developmental rather than magical concepts. The work, as distinct from the emotional component of the group (see Basic assumptions) is geared to a task but one never occurs without the other.

Erratum

p.74. The last three lines of the paragraph under the heading – **Transference** should be deleted and the following substituted:

> develop in a looser sense multipersonally or multilaterally. Counter transference is the therapist's transference to the patient or to the patient's transference.

Recommended Further Reading

There are literally many hundreds of books on the subject of 'group psychotherapy'. We feel it appropriate to limit our recommendations for further study of the subject to the following short list. We are fully aware of the excellence of many other books, but cannot do justice to the whole field.

Shorter Books

Group Psychotherapy, by S. H. Foulkes and E. J. Anthony. Penguin Books, 1957 and 1965. [Probably the best introduction to small group psychotherapy, but theoretical chapters tend to be demanding.]

Small Group Psychotherapy, Edited by H. Walton. Penguin Books, 1971. [An excellent concise introduction to the subject.]

Experiences in Groups, by W. R. Bion. Tavistock Publications, 1961. [A fascinating, intensely personal account of Bion's original approach to groups.]

Perspectives in Group Psychotherapy, by P. B. de Mare. Allen and Unwin, 1972. [A philosophical over-view of the total group scene, demanding in parts.]

Textbooks

Group Psychotherapy and Group Function, Edited by M. Rosenbaum and M. Berger. Basic Books Inc., 1963. [An excellent comprehensive book of 690 pages, useful as a work of reference.]

The Theory and Practice of Group Psychotherapy, by I. D. Yalom. Basic Books Inc., 1970. [Another first-class textbook, beautifully written, packed with references.]

Journals

The International Journal of Group Psychotherapy. Published four times a year by the International University Press Inc., New York, on behalf of the American Group Psychotherapy Association. [The major journal devoted to group work, a 'must' for anyone wishing to keep up with developments in the theory and practice of group psychotherapy.]

Group Analysis: International Panel and Correspondence (GAIPAC). Published three times a year by the Chaucer Publishing Co. Ltd., on behalf of the Group-analytic Society, and Institute of Group-analysis (London). [An informed, highly-personal journal, edited by S. H. Foulkes, which encourages on-going discussion of a wide range of topics related to groups of all types. Enjoyable, provocative, and stimulating.]

Index